Awakening to the Spirit Within

Eight Paths

Pamela Smith Allen, Ph.D.

Foreword by Rev. Dr. Christian Sorensen

ISBN: 1-4107-3411-0 (e-book)
ISBN: 1-4140-2061-9 (Paperback)

Library of Congress Control Number: 2003091825

This book is printed on acid free paper.

Printed in the United States of America
Bloomington, IN

1stBooks - rev. 12/15/03

Dedication

To Annaliese, Ashley, Garrett, Graham, Hannah, and Jacob, in hopes that they, and the other children of the world, may someday experience peace on earth

In Loving Memory Of

Dora, Michael, Jeanie, and all of my family and friends who have made their transitions to the spirit side of life.

Acknowledgments

I am very grateful to Larry, for his support and encouragement, without which this book would never have been completed. I am grateful, not only for his understanding of my need to immerse myself in writing for extended periods of time, but also for his willingness to read and respond to each new chapter as it evolved. His feedback (while sometimes difficult to accept, especially in the beginning) was always honest and handed out with huge doses of love and support. I quickly learned that his suggestions really would improve the clarity of ideas which I wanted to present.

I am also grateful to my daughter, Kerry, for her support and involvement in this project (reading, editing, and suggesting possible graphics and cover design). I am also grateful to Kerry and Arlan for bringing my little granddaughter, Annaliese, into the world. I knew even before her birth that I wanted to dedicate this book to her, as well as to little Ashley, and the other children in my life.

I am grateful to my sister, Dianne, for her willingness to read the entire manuscript, and also for sharing it with her friends (particularly Barbara, who supported my efforts so much). I am also grateful to Dianne for her love and encouragement of my writing efforts over the years.

I want to thank my friend and advisor, Ted Melnechuk, for encouraging me to write this book and for sending me such helpful resources over the years. I am also grateful to Bob Lee for taking the time to send encouragement and resources from Canada.

Another person who deserves recognition is my dear friend and yoga teacher, Ayosea, who read the manuscript and gave me such wonderful feedback and support. Ayosea also introduced me to Leslie, who made it possible for me to use the book as a teaching tool with her advanced yoga teacher trainees. I am grateful to Leslie and members of that very first class (Bobbie, Christa, Monique, and Rekina), for allowing me such a wonderful opportunity. I am also grateful to Susan, who encouraged me to use the book as a teaching tool.

I now want to acknowledge some special people who read individual chapters from the manuscript and offered valuable feedback. My gratitude is extended to Mel, for her input regarding Chapter Six, as well as for her editorial expertise; to Maura, for her wisdom as a teacher and friend, as well as for her feedback regarding Chapter Five; to Ruti, for her willingness to read and offer feedback regarding Chapter Four; and to Genie, for reading Chapter One and allowing me to tell the story of Michael and the gifts he left us both. To the women of my "group" (Batya, Deborah, Maura, Paulette, and Ruth), gratitude is extended for their support of my writing efforts and for providing the perfect arena for applying spiritual ideas and concepts to daily life.

I would now like to express my gratitude to Rev. Dr. Christian Sorensen, for writing the foreword to this book and also for providing such wonderful spiritual guidance over the years. Christian also put me in touch with a wonderful literary agent (Barbara Neighbors Deal), who educated me in how to prepare a professional-looking manuscript. Believing in the merits of the book, she was tireless in her efforts to send it to potential publishers. Barbara was also responsible for introducing me to 1st Books Library. This provided another possibility for completing the publication process. Truly, there are no accidents - only opportunities. Thanks also to Rhett Miller, for enhancing and preparing the graphics for insertion into each chapter heading.

I now want to acknowledge some of the other wonderful teachers and friends, whose wisdom and guidance through the years helped inspire me to write this book: Gerald Ice, Patty O'Dea, Ray Jordan, Joan Sigurdson, Joe

Gustin, Barbara Roberts, George Emery, Sheldon Kramer, Mark Siegrist, Brother Ishmael Tetteh, and Sister Esta Tetteh. I am also grateful to my "non-physical" spiritual teachers, whose guidance contributed so much to my life and to the writing of this book.

With regard to 1st Books Library, I am very grateful to Margaret Burns for so promptly and thoroughly introducing me to this wonderful, cutting-edge manner of publishing and also for assisting me in preparing the book for submission. I am also very grateful to Teri Watkins and Joanie Trisler for seeing to the many details involved in producing this book. Thanks to Patrick East for making himself available for questions and concerns and to all the staff at 1st Books Library who participated in creating the cover design, format, and finished project.

Even though their names may not be mentioned here, I want to thank all of my family, extended family, and friends, for their continued support and encouragement, as well as for understanding when I needed to be absent from their midst in order to complete this project (particularly Mark, who wondered why I missed so many Friday night gatherings). To those who live far away, I am very grateful that they remembered so often to ask me how the book was coming along. That meant more to me than they will ever know.

Contents

Foreword

(by Rev. Dr. Christian Sorensen)

In this book, Pamela Allen has explored eight spiritual pathways. Although they are framed within different sacred traditions, each points to the Divine Spirit which exists within all human beings, regardless of the culture from which they come.

As Spiritual Community Leader of the United Church of Religious Science, world-wide, and Senior Minister of Seaside Church in Encinitas, California, I am pleased that Dr. Allen has included the New Thought Movement as one of the eight pathways discussed in her book. In my opinion, this movement uniquely blends western scientific principles with eastern mystical teachings.

I am also pleased that Dr. Allen has addressed the sense of separation and alienation which so many people feel in the world today, not only within the communities in which they live, but also deep within themselves. As a psychologist and teacher, she has assisted her clients and students in recognizing and appreciating who they are as individuals. She admits, however, that psychology and education are limited when it comes to addressing deeper spiritual needs. I have met many people throughout the world who suffer from the spiritual hunger, to which Dr. Allen refers, and agree with her that it is important to help people identify avenues for exploring the deeper needs of their souls.

While it is important to have the freedom to explore the divinity within oneself, it is also helpful to have a spiritual framework, as well as a teacher or guide, to assist in this process. If one of the pathways described in this book appeals to you, I would advise you to seek out a spiritual community which offers the guidance and support you will need as you immerse yourself in its practices.

It is evident that the eight paths Dr. Allen discusses have been a part of her own spiritual journey. This is exemplified by the personal reflections which are included in each chapter. It is also evident that she has read widely and done scholarly research in bringing this valuable information to us.

The combination of personal experiences and clear, concise presentation of key points makes for enjoyable and informative reading about a subject which has great relevance, not only for those of us involved in the New Thought Movement, but for anyone who aspires to evolve as a spiritual being and to join others around the world in bringing a greater sense of peace and harmony to our planet.

In Love
Rev. Christian Sorensen
8-31-01

Preface

Like other freedom-loving citizens of the United States of America and throughout the world, I am deeply saddened by the terrorist attacks which took place in New York, Washington D.C. and Pennsylvania on September 11, 2001. These events painfully point out the need for cooperative endeavors to facilitate understanding and peaceful coexistence among the many groups of people who share our planet. It is time in our evolution as human beings to find ways of healing the emotional wounds of people all around the globe. I believe that one of the ways in which this may be done is by learning to appreciate the various religious pathways in existence in different parts of the world and by gleaning from these pathways some of the universal truths which may be used to help us learn to live in peace.

Unfortunately, many of the religions in our world, when interpreted in a rigid, fanatical manner, have been used to promote separation and alienation rather than connection and harmony. Not only was this the case in the recent terrorist events, but also in the violent wars which have been fought on this planet throughout history. Even though the major prophets of our world's religions taught a loving acceptance of all people, there are still those who would use the very religions which developed out of their teachings as an excuse to verbally and physically attack those whose views differ from their own. The recent shootings in our nation's schools painfully highlight the ever-growing need in our own country to promote tolerance of differences in our children so that a peaceful future will be possible for them.

It has been my purpose in writing this book to provide you with a short introduction to eight sacred pathways which have developed from various cultures around the world. Why eight paths? One reason is that I have been drawn to each of them at one time or another in my own life and the other is that the numeral, eight, when turned on its side, is the symbol of infinity. Indeed, let us seek to connect with that Spirit which is infinite within ourselves and which unites us all, regardless of the outer form of our chosen religious practices.

Pamela Smith Allen
October 4, 2001
San Marcos, CA

Introduction

Introduction

This book is about coming to know ourselves from the inside out rather than the outside in. In other words, it is about discovering the Spirit which exists deep within the core of all human beings, regardless of gender, age, culture, race, religion, or any other identity with which they might be identified. This Spirit Within is constantly present in our lives, though most people are not aware of its existence except under extraordinary circumstances.

The eight paths described in this book offer possible avenues to the spiritual voyager by which the Spirit Within may be discovered. The destination is not so important as the journey itself, for, at any time along the way, one may awaken to that which has always been present deep within. The Spirit Within may also be referred to as the True Self, for it represents that which is natural and authentic to one's soul.

Each of the eight paths introduced in this book embraces the notion that there is no one right way to approach spirituality. Different approaches work best with different people. This is a view shared by many spiritual teachers and authors in the world today.

As the spokes of a wheel are essential for its turning, each living creature on our planet has a role to play in the sacred circle of life. Increasing technological advances in our world have brought people from different countries and cultures closer together than ever before. To use computer language, we are all part of a "world-wide web." What affects one part of the web also affects the rest. If we are to survive as a human race, we must learn to respect and appreciate one another's views about who we are and why we are here on this planet. This is essential if we are to evolve spiritually to a degree that peace on earth is truly possible.

In my own spiritual journey, I have been drawn to those sacred pathways which tend to be mystical in nature. Unlike some of the more traditional religions, mystical pathways emphasize communion with that which is Divine within oneself. Mystics tend to use a direct approach by going within themselves and asking the important questions of life. In addition, they trust that they will receive answers to their questions. This may come through the receiving of visual images, dreams, the words of a song, or through a chance meeting with just the right person at just the right time.

In today's world, I have met many people who are searching for a meaningful framework in which to explore themselves as human beings. Hoping to navigate more effectively through this stressful and chaotic world, they seek ways to feel connected with something greater than themselves which will offer a strong sense of inner peace. Much healing is needed in the world today. This healing is needed in individual lives, in communities, and among the nations of our world.

Since the mystical approach is *inner-directed*, it allows for individual differences in how the Divine is approached and acknowledged. Teachers from mystical pathways are not there to tell anyone what is right and what is wrong, but, rather, to help individuals to discover these truths within themselves.

It is possible that the more traditional forms of religion have failed to meet your spiritual longings and you are searching for a pathway which will have greater meaning and relevance for you. On the other hand, you may be content with your present spiritual pathway, while also wanting to increase your knowledge of other traditions. You may be feeling a need to understand someone in your life who adheres to one of the paths discussed in this book or you may be seeking ways to enhance your present practice with some of the techniques available from other spiritual traditions.

In my own quest for inner peace, I have traveled down a number of different pathways. As a psychologist, I have been exposed to many therapeutic interventions which have been very helpful but which are limited when it comes to addressing the deeper needs of the soul. The eight pathways included in this book, however, do address these deeper spiritual needs. It has been my purpose to provide you with a short introduction to these paths and to share with you some of my own personal experiences with them.

Although the eight paths appear to be different in form, there are threads of similarity running through them. It is my belief that their teachings create beautiful designs around the periphery of a common center point, from which the Infinite Spirit breathes individual expressions of life. Some of these threads of similarity are woven together for you in the conclusion. In addition, I have pointed out some of the unique gifts from each path.

In order to make the reading a bit more personal, I have included some of my own experiences with each of the pathways as well as spiritual guidance I have received along my own personal journey to the Divine within myself.

As we discover that the Divine is approachable within ourselves, life becomes a classroom, filled with new challenges and opportunities to grow in our own awareness and to help shed light on the pathways of others, who are ready to make their own inner pilgrimages. The sacred journey leads us back home to our natural state, which is divine and beautiful. When we embark on such a journey, light inner garments replace heavy outer clothing as we become free of ego entanglements no longer necessary. Excess baggage is released along the way so that we may travel more easily along the pathway to ourselves. As old life patterns are released, new patterns emerge, fueled by spiritual energy from a Divine Source. By returning to ourselves, we create a more harmonious and sacred circle of life.

By living from the inside out, rather than the outside in, we are empowered by the Spirit Within to make a difference in the world. We come to realize that the center of who we are has no beginning and no end. It is a sacred circle within us which connects us to everything in the world and also to a power which I believe encompasses us all. Some refer to this power as God or as The Source. Some refer to it as Universal Intelligence. I like to use the term, Infinite Spirit.

All of these sacred paths are designed to lead you, the seeker, to the Divine Spirit which exists within you. Therefore, I encourage you to be open and receptive to your own inner guidance and creativity as you travel through the pages of this book toward ever-increasing feelings of wholeness and inner peace. There are practice exercises in each chapter to help you in this respect. If you wish to go into greater depth in any of the pathways, it is suggested that you connect with a spiritual teacher and a community which will give you support and guidance. There are also many references and suggested readings offered at the end of the book. No doubt the Internet is a good resource as well. And now, may you have a wonderful journey discovering that which is Divine in you.

Chapter One

Native American Spirituality

While traveling down the path of Native American Spirituality, we become attuned to the lessons available to us through our interaction with the natural environment. By appreciating and aligning with the spiritual forces in nature, we become empowered, from the ground up, so to speak, to live more natural and authentic lives.

Native American Spirituality

The Medicine Path

It has been said that the indigenous tribes of the world are Mother Earth's caretakers. In the light of the destruction of our planet which goes on every minute of every day, we have much to learn from these caretakers, who understand the ways of living in harmony with nature. Since this book is written on American soil, it seems appropriate to begin with a discussion of a spiritual pathway which is integral to the Native American way of life, often referred to as the Medicine Path.

The word, medicine, in the context of the Medicine Path, refers to those things which are spiritually enhancing to one's life experience. For instance, prayers and sacred ceremonies would be considered by Native Americans to be "good medicine." The Medicine Path, in some parts of the world, may also be referred to as the path of shamans.

Although some Native Americans do not feel comfortable sharing their spiritual practices with non-natives, other spiritual leaders in the Native American community have a different viewpoint. They feel that the time has come to share these sacred ceremonies in order to help promote world peace and to heal the environment.

Ed McGaa's book, *Mother Earth Spirituality,* is an excellent resource for gaining an appreciation of some of the spiritual traditions practiced by the Lakota. My own teacher, Gerald Ice, is another native traditional who has been active in teaching non-natives some of the Native American ways. Ice and McGaa have indicated that this will help to educate the people on our planet to live in harmony with Mother Earth. They believe that non-natives who are sincere in their belief in Great Spirit and who follow native teachings appropriately may benefit from learning to use these practices.

2

They have also encouraged other traditionalists to share sacred teachings with both natives and non-natives alike.

The spiritual practices of the Lakota, or Sioux, have been written about by many Native American authors, including Ed McGaa, who tells us that the Lakota name for Great Spirit is Wakan Tanka. According to the Lakota, Wakan Tanka is the creator of the universe. In addition, all of Wakan Tanka's creations are interconnected. It is important, according to the Lakota, to honor and respect all of these creations so that peace and harmony on the planet may exist.

The Lakota believe that spirits are present all around us. These spirits, overseen by Wakan Tanka, are available to help people in times of need and may be called upon for assistance by way of special ceremonies which have been created for this purpose.

A modern spiritual teacher and author, Don Miguel Ruiz, has written a very popular and practical book, entitled *The Four Agreements*, which imparts ancient Toltec wisdom he learned from his mother and grandfather. Ruiz feels that it is time for this ancient wisdom to be shared with the world at large so that we may work to create more harmony and beauty in the world. Many people are finding his teachings to be extremely helpful to them as they travel along their spiritual pathways.

When I was asked to choose a culture to study as part of a psychology class in multi-cultural family counseling, I chose the Native American culture. Since I was living near an Indian reservation at the time, I interviewed some people from that particular reservation, as well as others who lived in an urban area near by. They told me of the importance of stories, songs, myths, and symbols, in passing on spiritual principles to their children. I later read Hyemeyohsts Storm's book, *Seven Arrows*. The material spoke to my heart and I knew it was important for me to learn as much as I could about Native American teachings.

As a psychologist, I am interested in the healing process. Medicine men and women around the world utilize natural plants and herbs to treat illnesses of a physical, as well as psychological nature. Shamanism has been practiced in many tribal cultures around the world and is now being taught to non-natives who also want to explore this natural form of healing.

In Shamanism, the sound of drumming or rattling is often used as part of the healing process. The shaman, lying down next to the client, may take a journey deep within the spiritual world in order to gain valuable information which will prove beneficial to the person seeking assistance. Perhaps a spirit animal will be discovered and brought back in a psychic sense to help the person deal with life in a more powerful and effective way. Perhaps the underlying cause of a particular physical ailment and its cure will be discovered by the shaman in this process.

Utilization of the mind to aid in the healing process is now being accepted by physicians and other healers as an important ingredient in treating illnesses. This is opening the door once again to the use of holistic methods such as shamanism. For those of you interested in learning more about this practice, it is suggested that you read *The Way of the Shaman*, written by Michael Harner.

The Vision Quest
(Crying for a Vision)

A very important Native American spiritual ceremony is the Vision Quest. The purpose of a Vision Quest is to ask Great Spirit for a vision or dream which will demonstrate the higher purpose for a person's life. The Vision Quest usually begins with a cleansing, sometimes composed of a fast and a Sweat Lodge Ceremony. Participants may climb a hill or go to a secluded place before dark and sit or lie down on a blanket by themselves for the entire evening. The next morning, they go back to camp and share their visions, dreams, and other experiences with one another.

One of the greatest Native American visionaries was Black Elk. In a vision, he saw four horses - red, yellow, black, and white. The colors of the horses later came to represent the four directions as well as four races of people on earth. Black Elk knew that each race had special gifts to bring to the world. (See *Black Elk Speaks,* by John Neirhart, for more information about this remarkable holy man and the gifts he gave to the Lakota nation.)

Even though I have not gone on a traditional Vision Quest, as described in Native Americans writings, I have spent many hours in the out-of-doors, observing the natural world and learning from these experiences. Being a part of nature, indeed, embraced by nature, may be a very healing experience. For example, during the pain of going through a divorce, I found comfort, as well as strength, in observing the ocean waves as they broke on the shore and then retreated back out to sea. Observing the wind as it changed from a gentle breeze into a storm helped me to understand my own emotions during that difficult time in my life. On one occasion, I saw the sun shining radiant streams through a dark cloud. I wrote in my journal that the light is always there, even when things seem to be dark. I knew in my heart that trusting God would bring the light through those dark experiences in my life.

Living out in the country near an Indian Reservation for about five years gave me a wonderful opportunity to be embraced by nature and, in the process, to understand myself more fully. I found myself writing poetry in an attempt to describe metaphorically that which nature was teaching me. If I had been a painter, I would have painted it. Poetry, however, was the vehicle which worked best for me.

Visions and dreams are greatly honored on the Native American spiritual path. I have discovered that, in addition to going on an external

Vision Quest, one may also go on an internal Vision Quest. By using meditation and visualization, for example, it is possible to become receptive to the inner images and sounds within oneself, which may be helpful in determining one's purpose or direction in life.

As a psychologist, I was trained to use visualization and guided imagery as a therapeutic tool with my clients. It was a natural step for me to begin to use these tools with myself as I explored the inner planes of my own consciousness. In my travels along the Medicine Path, I naturally brought some of my experiences with visualization and guided imagery into play.

Working with meditation and visualization, I was able to go on mental Vision Quests, imagining myself in very special and secluded places, and then asking to receive visions and messages which would be for my highest and best good. In these sessions, I began to receive visual images and auditory messages which were helpful to me in determining the direction my life would take. At first, the "messengers" appeared in animal form, then later, as a Native American guide.

When I first began to receive inner messages, I thought of them as "just my imagination." Then I began to realize that imagination is one of the most important mind functions available to human beings. Without it, many wonderful inventions would never have come into fruition. I came to understand that the images and messages I receive during periods of meditation and receptivity are from a higher place in my consciousness, where it is possible to tap into inner wisdom. I have since taken intuitive development classes with Spiritualist teachers who believe that all people have spirit guides available to them for various purposes in life such as protection, inspiration, and instruction.

Whether messages comes from entities in non-physical realms or from our own higher selves, my experience has taught me that spiritual guidance is available at any time to anyone who is open to the possibility of receiving it. The form in which it comes, however, depends on the framework of the recipient. For example, Catholics may perceive their inner guides in the form of Christian saints, whereas Hindus may perceive their guides in the form of Hindu deities. My own inner guidance has come through many different forms, depending on my frame of reference at the time. For example, when I was exploring Vision Quests, an inner guide appeared to me in Native American form. I have included some of the messages I received because they represent the kind of inner guidance we have been discussing.

The image was a tipi (tee-pee). The message was:

"The tipi is very sacred. There's an opening at the top. As the smoke from the fire rises to the Sky Father, so our spirits soar. Entering the tipi through the door in front is like entering the womb of Earth Mother, to rest in her safety and be born again next day."

The following messages had to do with freedom:

"Freedom is only possible in the mind. You can never be free in the body from the cares of the world. Only in your mind can you soar freely through the light, above the cares of the world. Therefore, keep your mind clear and free and it can lift your spirit up where it longs to be. This can happen at any time, in any place. That, you will see, is freedom."

"Rise up above your pain and turmoil. Look toward the light. It will transport you to a new place, a place of peace and quiet, a place for new beginnings, far away from the pain and turmoil which slowly disappears from your memory."

The image was an eagle, circling counter-clockwise up to the top of a hill. The message was:

"Sometimes Brother Eagle must go to a lonely spot on top of the hill to clear his head and see clearly what he must do. Like him, you must sometimes circle around until you see the lonely spot on top of the hill. There you can rise up and gain a clearer perspective. Your heart is in the right place, but your senses are scattered. Bring your senses into harmony with your heart. When you are all together in one piece on top of the hill, you will see clearly what you must do."

The image was the setting sun. The message was:

"As the sun is setting on the world, tune in to the night creatures. They too have spirits and are here to help you along your pathway. Mother Earth has many lessons to teach you, just as Father Sky and Grandfather Sun have many lessons for you. Mother Earth provides a foundation for you and Father Sky offers spiritual awareness. You form a bridge between the two. One inspires and the other manifests. You are the medium between the two. Be a wise medium and stay in balance."

I was shown a feather. The message was:

"Each part of the feather grows outward from a common stem. Your essence is the stem. The feathery branches are all the parts of you which, together, make up the whole. Your task is to bring them all into harmony. The stem holds them all together, but the parts define its character. So it is in all phases of life."

The following messages had to do with children:

"Teach kids how to balance out their lives and come into harmony with the earth."

"Look to nature and to that which is natural in the children's faces when they are truly being themselves. When they are not, help remove the obstacles to this natural expression."

"Give the children hope. Touch the sacred place inside of them so that they know who they are, and touch those who teach and

parent them in a way that they, too, give the children hope, for a lighted future."

The Sweat Lodge Ceremony

(A Ceremony for Cleansing and Prayer)

A few years ago, I saw a poster in one of the schools where I worked, advertising that Gerald Ice, a Lakota spiritual leader, would be lecturing in one of the hotels in that area on the following evening. Because of my increasing interest in the Medicine Path, I decided to attend this lecture. When I heard the drumming and singing and smelled the fragrant aroma of burning sage which filled the air, I knew I was in for a treat.

During his lecture, Gerald told the Lakota legend of Buffalo Calf Woman. She was a beautiful Indian maiden who appeared in a vision to two native men, one who lusted after her and the other who revered her as a spirit. The one who lusted after her was destroyed and the one who revered her as a spirit introduced her to his tribe.

According to Gerald's telling of the story, Buffalo Calf Woman brought with her a bundle which contained a sacred clay pipe. This pipe would, thereafter, be incorporated into many spiritual ceremonies which she taught the people. According to the legend, after teaching these ceremonies, the beautiful woman turned into a white buffalo calf and returned to the spirit world. One of the ceremonies which she gave to the people was the Sweat Lodge. This is a cleansing ceremony which also involves reconnecting with Mother Earth. Prayers are lifted in the lodge to Great Spirit, offering thanks and asking for protection and guidance.

After hearing Gerald's description of the Sweat Lodge, I decided to sign up for one. In preparation, our group collected lava rocks, which were referred to as "stone people." We gathered them from the desert during a

9

special outing. They were the stones to be used in the Sweat Lodge. In addition, our group was instructed in the making of prayer ties, which were to be an important part of the ceremony as well. We purchased pure tobacco that had not been treated in any way. We also purchased string and 100% cotton material (black, white, red, yellow). The colors represented the four directions. Some people also bought green and blue material to represent Mother Earth and Father Sky. We said personal prayers as we placed the tobacco in small squares and then tied them together into a formation similar to a kite string. These were called "prayer ties."

When the day of the Sweat Lodge arrived, I meditated and asked for guidance which would help me to participate as fully as possible in the ceremony. The following message came:

> *"The Sweat Lodge is for all the people - to bring them back into harmony with Mother Earth and with each other. It is for the ancestors, the people of today, and the children of tomorrow, as well as for yourself."*

The dome which served as the Sweat Lodge was made of branches that had been covered with blankets. In the middle of the lodge, a pit had been dug to hold hot stones, which were heated outside over a fire. The women in our group wore cotton dresses and no cosmetics. (Wearing cosmetics would have caused our skin to burn.) The men wore cotton shorts. We were all barefoot. Women participating in the sweat lodge were not supposed to be "in their moon time" (menstruating). Moon time is considered a special time when women are going through their own purification process, which is very powerful. To participate in a Sweat Lodge or any other sacred event at this time, I was told, would be to interfere with the calling of spirits by the leader of the sweat lodge. Diana Steer, in her book, *Native American Women*, explains this in more detail. You may want to read her book for more information regarding the roles women play in many Native American cultures.

Outside our Sweat Lodge was an altar, upon which certain foods had been placed, as an offering to the spirits. Special objects, such as feathers or crystals, were also placed on the altar, to be blessed during the ceremony. Our prayer ties were placed in the lodge so that the prayers would be amplified by the ceremony. We entered the lodge in a ceremonial manner and sat in a circle. The leader sat near the entrance.

After a period of quiet in the dark lodge, the fire tender brought in the first four stones. When the water was poured on them, the steam rose up and the lodge became intensely hot. This is when I had to hide my face in a wet towel and cool my nostrils by smelling a piece of sweet sage.

There were four rounds in which stones were brought in and steam was created. Between rounds, a flap of the dome was raised to let in a little cool air. The experience was deeply ceremonial and spiritual, with much raising of prayers to Wakan Tanka and honoring of Mother Earth. Prayers for peace and healing of the planet were said, as well as prayers for wisdom and spiritual knowledge. We also sang. Even though I did not know the Lakota words, the melodies were hauntingly beautiful and served as a medium for connecting me in spirit to the ancestors who had sung these songs for centuries.

During one of the rounds, individual prayers were said out loud, one at a time, around the circle. At the end of every prayer, the phrase, *Mitakuye Oyasin* (for all my relatives) was usually said. Remembering the message I had received prior to this experience, I gave thanks for the opportunity to be allowed to participate in the Sweat Lodge, even though I was not a native, and prayed that the children of tomorrow would live in peace and harmony together. Others prayed for personal guidance and also for peace on the planet. After we left the lodge, we gathered outside for a Pipe Ceremony.

The pipe had been filled with tobacco in a ceremonial manner. I knew from Gerald's lectures that the sacred pipe was representative of peace. The bowl, a feminine symbol, was made of red clay, representing Mother Earth. The stem, a masculine symbol, was made of wood, representing growing things. Gerald had emphasized the importance of honoring both feminine and masculine energies in life so that they would work together to balance each other.

During the Pipe Ceremony, the six directions (East, West, North, South, Sky Above, and Earth Below) were honored and the pipe was passed around. We smoked for peace on earth and prosperity for all the people. The smoke lifted our prayers up to Great Spirit. The ashes were sprinkled on the ground and the pipe was put away.

The experience brought me in touch with Mother Earth, as well as Great Spirit. I felt a bond with the people in the lodge and also with the ancestors who had entered lodges such as this for many, many years prior to my own experience. Going to a Sweat Lodge is, for Native Americans, like going to church, in the real sense of the word. It is a sacred time of prayer and communion, as well as a time for cleansing and celebration.

If you are interested in attending a Sweat Lodge, I would suggest that you look for a leader who is Native American or has been trained in native practices, especially if you want to have a traditional experience. Each aspect of preparation and the ceremony itself is very sacred and should be treated as such.

The Medicine Wheel
(Living in Harmony)

Traditionally, in Native American tribes, elders have gathered together in circles, for the purpose of solving problems. In some cases, during these circle times, the "talking stick" (an object one holds when it is his or her turn) is passed around so that each person has an opportunity to speak to a particular issue. Since each individual is part of the whole, all opinions matter. This sacred circle has been called a Medicine Wheel.

There are sacred places around the world where people have gathered together to pray for thousands of years. Circular structures, resembling Medicine Wheels, have been found in many of these places. In England, for example, it is said that Stonehenge is probably such a place. At Stonehenge, stone structures have been created in a circular pattern, in harmony with the rotation of the earth around the sun.

In his book, *The Medicine Way: A Shamanic Path to Self Mastery*, Kenneth Meadows writes about some of the archaeological discoveries made in New England, which appear to be Celtic in origin. No one knows for sure how the Celts could have gotten to this country approximately 3000 years ago, but there are indications that they lived and practiced their religion here, alongside the Native American tribes in existence at that time. History tells us that the Celts from Britain and Northern Europe practiced a religion similar to that of the Native Americans, in that it was very harmonious with the cycles of nature.

The Medicine Wheel has much to offer our world with regard to the art of living in harmony with one another. Sun Bear, in his book, *The Medicine Wheel: Earth Astrology*, reports that he received a special vision from Great Spirit. It was a Medicine Wheel which would be shared with persons of all races. As a result of his vision, he founded a multiracial tribe, called the Bear Tribe, to promote the teachings of this kind of Medicine Wheel. It was depicted as a circle of life in which everyone and everything had a special place as well as unique gifts to bring forth for the benefit of all. The belief of the Bear Tribe is that the nations of the world need to learn to live in harmony with one another in order to bring things into balance, and that

13

Medicine Wheel ceremonies may be helpful in promoting this end. Sun Bear was careful to point out that his system was revealed to him spiritually and is not the same as a more traditional Native American system. More traditional ceremonies, he points out, should be carefully overseen by qualified spiritual leaders.

Kenneth Meadows, in his book, *Earth Medicine: A Shamanic Way to Self Discovery*, writes about an Earth Wheel, similar to the Medicine Wheel described by Sun Bear. Meadows had studied with a number of Native Americans teachers, including Wallace Black-Elk, as well as with various shamans in Europe. He developed a system for using this sacred circle for self development and growth. Meadows suggests that people might construct these wheels and walk around them, contemplating the qualities associated with each part. He also suggests that working with the wheel is like working with one's own mind.

Unlike astrological charts and signs, which remind us of how we are connected to the stars, the symbols used by Sun Bear, Meadows, and others remind us of how we are connected to Mother Earth. It is suggested that people born at certain times of the year are influenced by whatever seasonal characteristics are in existence at that time. These seasons are represented in the different directions depicted on the Medicine Wheel. By traveling around the wheel, symbolically, and interacting with people who were born under different seasonal influences, people may learn to respect and appreciate one another's gifts.

In general, those born in the spring are said to have been born on the eastern section of the Medicine Wheel. This location represents new beginnings and awakenings. It is often symbolized by an eagle. People who are born in the spring, according to this teaching, tend to have a keen sense of vision like the eagle. Vision is important if an overview of a particular situation is needed in order to make necessary changes. Although the colors of the directions are not always the same in different tribal ceremonies, the color red is often used to depict the east. It is the color of the rising sun.

The south section of the Medicine Wheel represents the place of summer. This direction is often symbolized by a coyote. People born during the summer months, according to this teaching, tend to be playful like a coyote. Other attributes of the south are innocence and trust. Some consider this direction to be the place of the inner child, which is playful, while also being wise in its close proximity to the natural, or spiritual state, of human beings. A color often associated with the south is yellow, which depicts the sun at noon-time.

The western portion of the Medicine Wheel represents the place of autumn. Autumn is a time of harvest. It is also a time just before winter, when the leaves begin to change in many parts of the world. The bear often symbolizes the west on Native American Medicine Wheels. People born in the west, according to this teaching, tend to be able to use contemplation as a tool for becoming more self aware. Like the bear, who seeks out a cave to use for hibernating through the winter, we must sometimes go inward and be alone with ourselves in order to discover who we really are. Black is often used to depict the west in accordance with the idea of going inside one's inner cave.

The north section of the Medicine Wheel represents the place of winter and is associated with wisdom. White depicts the north for it represents the snow in winter as well as the way our hair changes as we grow older. In native tribes, elders are revered as wise men and women. Many people born in the north on the Medicine Wheel may decide to become teachers. I, myself, was born in December and have spent much of my life as a teacher. The buffalo, which gives itself to the people so that they may have food and shelter, is often used to symbolize the north.

It is interesting that Black Elk's vision, as described earlier, included the four colors - red, yellow, black, and white, not only as colors of the four directions but also as colors of four races on earth. As a sacred circle, it is a tool for growing in awareness of oneself and others in the circle of life.

Concluding Comments

In this chapter, we discussed Native American spiritual practices, often referred to as the Medicine Path. We focused primarily on Lakota teachings, but also discussed more general practices of Native Americans which have been designed to promote healing and self empowerment. Some of the key points brought out in this chapter, which generally reflect the philosophical stance of many Native Americans, include the following:

> *There is a Great Spirit which holds everything in the universe together.*

> *It is possible to draw power and assistance from Great Spirit and also from spiritual guidance available on the inner planes of our awareness.*

> *It is very important to show gratitude to Great Spirit for the gifts of life we have received. The Sweat Lodge is a ceremony in which prayers of gratitude may be offered to Great Spirit.*

> *Everything in life has a spiritual essence which underlies its being.*

> *The Medicine Wheel Ceremony is a way of honoring the importance of each person in the circle of life and of promoting harmony within ourselves and with one another. This is essential if peace on our planet is to be achieved.*

It is important to recognize, respect, honor, and see the sacred aspects of all of creation, including plants, animals, minerals, and human beings.

Masculine and feminine energies, when in balance, complement one another creating harmony on our planet.

Personal Reflections

In reflecting on my experiences with Native American Spirituality, I am aware of how my appreciation for nature has been heightened and expanded in such a way that I feel more connected to my environment and more an integral part of all that makes up the world around me. I feel more at home, so to speak, on Mother Earth.

During my internal Vision Quests, I was fortunate in receiving helpful inner guidance. It is amazing that, in addition to being part of a physical environment, human beings are also part of an ever-expanding inner landscape, with images, sounds, and important lessons to learn. It's comforting to know that there are inner teachers, as well as teachers in the physical realm, to provide the guidance that we all need from time to time.

My participation in the Sweat Lodge Ceremony was profound and very sacred. Not only did I feel a strong connection with Mother Earth, but I also felt connected to Native American ancestors who have participated in these ceremonies since ancient times. Strangely, I felt a sense of connection to future generations as well, knowing that there would be others participating in such ceremonies in times to come. I knew in my heart of hearts that Great Spirit had received our prayers and was fully present in the lodge with each one of us.

My interest in the Medicine Wheel led me, a few years ago, to participate in a monthly women's group known as *Crones in Training*. We were a group of women who all shared an interest in Medicine Wheel gatherings. In these gatherings, we sat on the floor. The four directions were represented in our circle by four small sculptures (Eagle in the east, Coyote in the south, Bear in the west and Buffalo in the north). The Spirit above and Earth below were also honored.

Prior to entering the circle, we smudged and cleansed ourselves with burnt sage which had been gathered from Mother Earth. Tobacco or corn meal had been scattered on the ground before the sage was picked, as a token of appreciation to Mother Earth. On at least one occasion, the Medicine Wheel leader took us on an inner journey to meet our "totem animal." According to the Native American tradition, totem animals are considered to be spirit allies which are present on the inner planes of our minds and are available to us for support and guidance. You may read more about them in the book, *Medicine Cards,* by Jamie Sams and David Carson. Sams and Carson have created beautiful cards, with animals pictured on them, which may be used for identifying your totem animals and also for various kinds of self growth experiences.

Usually, in our Medicine Wheel gatherings, a talking stick was passed around after we had experienced a guided journey. Each person holding the talking stick had the floor and could share whatever she wanted to share about her journey. Participants would take turns sharing or had the option to pass the stick to the next person in the circle. Songs were sung and drums played. Everything was done with great reverence and appreciation.

My experience with Medicine Wheel gatherings has given me a wonderful frame of reference for viewing the experiences in my life. In these gatherings, I have truly felt the connectedness which exists between physical and spiritual realms. The Medicine Wheel also illustrated to me how everything in life has a purpose and a place in the scheme of things. Each life experience and each relationship we have is important in our quest for wholeness. The following inner message, which I received during a time of major transition, relates to this theme.

> *"There are many openings and closings of doorways as you move through your life. You close one door in order to enter the next one. Let go of the past in order to move into the future. Nothing is lost. As you see, you are moving in a great circle, returning to the place where you began. When the circle is complete, you are whole. It is the nature of life to move in these circles."*

It has been important for me to travel around the Medicine Wheel of my life, integrating the wisdom, vision, playfulness, and contemplation, represented by the four directions on the wheel. These qualities have been demonstrated so clearly by people I have met along this pathway. Everyone on our planet has gifts to give. There is so much for us to learn from each other if we will only take the time to appreciate each other's gifts.

An example of someone who was born in the south part of the Medicine Wheel is my brother, Michael. Like the coyote, he was playful and loved being out in nature. Even when he was dying of lung cancer at the tender age of forty-four, he was somehow able to keep his sense of humor, flashing that wonderful smile of his, and lighting up the room, as well as the hearts of those of us in his presence.

I would like to tell you a story about the coyote symbol, which is related to my brother's death. Being skilled with wood, Michael had carved many Native American symbols, which were placed around the home which he shared with his wife, Genie. One of them was a coyote which stood on a shelf in the living room.

Just after Michael died and his body was taken out of the house, Genie and the hospice counselor were sitting on the hospital bed where Michael had lain during the latter stages of his illness. They were trying to console each other when all of a sudden, the wooden coyote, which was across the room from them, "leaped" across the room and landed at their feet. Obviously, they were quite startled by this.

Genie looked at the counselor and said "Did you see what I just saw?" The counselor said "I sure did. I guess Michael wanted to get our attention and let us know he is okay." Both of them laughed out loud and felt much more at ease, sensing that Michael's spirit was still alive and well, even though his body had been left behind. What a gift!

Although it was extremely painful to say good-bye to my brother, I am grateful for the wonderful gifts he gave me. From him I learned how beautiful it is to live a simple life in harmony with nature. Michael was truly at home when deep in the woods, surrounded by the natural environment. During his life, he spent many wonderful hours out on the river in home-built boats, fishing with hand-crafted lures. His life seemed to personify the teachings of Native American Spirituality.

Before Michael died, he gave his wife and the rest of our family another gift, which he had received while traversing back and forth between consciousness and unconsciousness, indeed between life and death. He told Genie that he had been invited to take a trip through the woods with a guide and about 60 other men on the following Sunday morning. On Saturday night before he went to sleep, he said to Genie, "I guess I'd better say good-bye to you since I'll be going on my trip through the woods tomorrow morning." The next morning Genie found that Michael had quietly died in his sleep, slipping away, no doubt, to keep his appointment in the woods.

What a beautiful image Michael had been given by Spirit to assist him in making the transition from his earthly life experience to the next one that lay before him. And what a beautiful gift he gave to his wife to help her in the letting go process. When she told the rest of the family what had happened, we were comforted in our deep grief, knowing that he was not alone and that he had gone to a place that he loves dearly.

As you explore Native American Spirituality it is important to be open to the positive visual images, messages, and intuitive nudges that can be invaluable in your spiritual walk through life. I have learned to trust those messages which evoke feelings of well being in my heart and which suggest ways of living my life in a more authentic, loving manner.

Practice Exercises

The following imagery exercises are similar to ones used in the Medicine Wheel gatherings of which I was a participant. They are also similar to visualizations I learned in my psychological training with Dr. Sheldon Kramer. I would suggest that you record them and listen while closing your eyes in order to journey inward. You might also take turns with a partner, one reading while the other takes the inner journey. Be sure to record your experiences in a journal for later processing.

#1 Meeting your spirit totem animal

It is a beautiful sunny day. The sky is a brilliant shade of blue. There are a few clouds overhead, making beautiful patterns in the sky. The breeze is blowing gently and the temperature is just right-not too warm and not too cool. You are walking down a lovely path in the meadow. The grass is green all around you and there are wild flowers growing along the edge of the path. Just ahead there is a little grove of trees, which forms a cooling shade or canopy from the warm sun. You walk over to the little grove and notice that your path moves slowly downward a bit beneath the cool branches. You can smell the soft earth below as you walk easily down the path, noticing that the sun is making dappled patches of light on the ground around you.

The branches of the trees are blowing gently in the breeze and they seem to be whispering to you a message of peace and love.

Suddenly ahead of you, you notice a particularly interesting tree which seems to beckon to you to sit in its shade and rest for a while against its trunk. You decide to follow your intuition and rest against the tree trunk for a short while.

As you sit in this beautiful place, feeling comfortable and peaceful inside, you ask to have a visit from your totem spirit animal. Then you notice an animal walking slowly out into the clearing in front of you. The animal does not seem to be afraid of you and you are very comfortable in its presence. Just sit observing the animal for a few minutes. What kind of animal is it? Is it large or small? What is it doing? What feelings does it arouse in you? If you like, you may ask your totem spirit animal if it has a message for you. (**Pause** long enough to do this.) *Now thank your animal friend for coming to you. See it gradually moving away, back into the trees from whence it came. Now count slowly from one to ten and, on the count of ten, come back to the place where you started this journey- one, two, three, four, five, six, seven, eight, nine, ten. Now move your fingers around a little and slowly open your eyes.*

#2 Meeting your spirit guide

It is a beautiful sunny day. The sky is a brilliant shade of blue. There are a few clouds overhead, making beautiful patterns in the sky. The breeze is blowing gently and the temperature is just right-not too warm and not too cool. You are walking down a lovely path in the meadow. The grass is green all around you and there are wild flowers growing along the edge of the path. Just ahead you see that your path is slowly moving upward along the side of a hill. The path is not too steep and you are able to walk on it with ease. As you slowly walk upward towards the top of the hill, you feel the breeze softly caress your face. You feel very comfortable and peaceful as you walk up the path.

Now you reach the top of the hill. The air smells fresh and clean as you take a deep breath and look all around you at the beautiful valley below. The colors are brilliant in the sunlight and you feel a sense of awe as you become aware of the beauty of this place. Feeling very much at peace inside, you sit down on a boulder in the shade of a tree. You then ask to see your spirit guide and notice someone coming over to see you from behind a large boulder not far away. Take time to notice as much as you can about your guide. Is it a male or female? How old is your guide? How is your guide dressed? Take time to ask a question of your guide. It might be a specific question. It might also be a general one, such as asking for a message for your highest and best good. Listen carefully. (Pause long enough to do this.) *Now thank your guide and begin to say good-bye. On the count of ten you will return to the place where you started this journey - one, two, three, four, five, six, seven, eight, nine, ten. Now move your fingers around a little and slowly open your eyes.*

Card Spreads

Use the *Medicine Cards* by Sams and Carson or the *Sacred Path Cards* by Sams, noted in the reference section. The *Medicine Cards* have beautiful pictures of animals on them and the *Sacred Path Cards* have pictures of Native American symbols. They may be used to ask specific or general questions about your life. There are many card spreads which are suggested in these books. Even when they are repeated, each experience will be different and special.

Medicine Wheel Gatherings

Create a Medicine Wheel with a group of people. Choose a place inside or outside for your sacred ceremony. Burn some sage in an abalone shell or a bowl and fan the smoke over your bodies in order to smudge, or cleanse yourselves, in preparation for the ceremony. Next honor the spirits and powers of the six directions (Father Sky-Above, Mother Earth-Below, Eagle-East, Coyote-South, Bear-West, and Buffalo-North). Express gratitude for the special gifts from each direction (guidance, nurturance, vision, playfulness, contemplation, and wisdom, respectively). Drumming or singing might be done at this point, or a drumming audio cassette could be played to set the mood for a guided journey. Choose a leader to read one of the two guided imagery exercises presented earlier for the whole group to experience. Afterwards, pass a talking stick around and relate your experiences with the group.

Receiving Gifts from Mother Earth

Take a walk in the woods or along a beautiful seashore. Stop to gather small objects which seem to call out to you. Items such as stones, feathers, shells, etc. may be gathered and placed in a "medicine pouch" which you may want to make or purchase to wear around your neck or around your waist. Remember to observe the lessons Mother Earth teaches you. Take along a journal to record your experiences. Don't forget to watch sunrises and sunsets for very special gifts of beauty and inspiration.

Attend Workshops and Seminars

Tribal groups often gather for pow-wows, some of which are open to the public. Enjoy the dances and beautiful crafts which are displayed at these gatherings. Check the Learning Annex, or similar magazines in your area, for workshops and seminars in your area.

Chapter Two
Taoism

While traveling down the Taoist path, we become aware of the receptive (yin) and expressive (yang) energies in nature. As we harmonize our lives with these energies, we become centered and true to ourselves, flowing naturally from one activity to another without losing our balance.

Taoism

The Tao

The Tao (pronounced "Dow") has been described by some authors as "the way." Originating in ancient China, it has also been referred to as "the source." I like to think of the Tao as the Infinite Spirit which holds everything together, something like the Great Spirit of Native American Spirituality discussed in the previous chapter.

The Tao may not be seen directly, but its effects may be seen, heard, and felt. It is that which controls the constantly changing cycles we see in nature. Taoism is a way of life which is in harmony with these cycles. According to this philosophy, it isn't the end of the journey which is important, but each step along the way. When meditating, for example, a Taoist does so for the sheer joy of it, rather than for the purpose of achieving anything. In other words, taking time to "smell the flowers" along one's journey, is a very Taoist way of living.

Many seekers have followed the path of the Tao in order to find peace in the midst of a chaotic world. Lao Tzu, in his famous *Tao te Ching*, presents ancient Taoist sayings which have inspired readers for many years to find peace within themselves as they "flow" from one event in their lives to another. In order to stay healthy, followers of the Tao are advised to harmonize themselves with nature and maintain a sense of balance in their lives. When human beings allow themselves to do this, they use the least amount of energy needed to deal with particular situations. In this way energy may be stored up for later use.

The Taoist concept of healing was explored by Bill Moyers, in a documentary for public television, entitled *Healing and the Mind, with Bill Moyers*. Moyers visited China and explored some of the Chinese healing practices which are based on the philosophy of Taoism. His guide was Dr. David Eisenberg, an American doctor and Harvard professor trained in Chinese medicine. Dr. Eisenberg took Moyers on a tour of Chinese hospitals where herbs, massage, acupuncture, and meditation were used to treat many chronic illnesses. Eisenberg discussed some of the ways in which western science and eastern healing methods are being blended into effective treatment options. He also took Moyers to the park to see how the people practiced Tai Chi Chuan in order to keep ch'i, which he defined as life energy, flowing smoothly in their bodies to maintain good health.

Yin and Yang

Taoists tell us that life energy (ch'i) circulates throughout the universe. Sometimes this energy is receptive (yin) and sometimes expressive (yang). According to the philosophy of Taoism, the yin and yang forces in nature, which were created from primordial ch'i, make up the world as we now know it. (See the yin/yang symbol at the beginning of this chapter.)

The yang, or white part of the yin/yang symbol, represents what many refer to as the masculine aspects of the Tao, while the yin, or black part of the symbol, represents what many refer to as the feminine aspects of the Tao. Both yin and yang energies, according to Taoism, exist in all people. Yin and yang do not literally refer to male or female qualities in terms of gender. They are, rather, aspects of energy which exist in both genders. According to Taoism, it is the interplay of these complementary aspects of ch'i which makes up our universe.

Yin and yang energies are said to complement, rather than compete with one another. Within yin, there is also the potential for yang. Within yang, there is also the potential for yin. This is represented by the small white dot in the dark side of the symbol and the small black dot in the white side of the symbol. Sickness, according to this philosophy, is caused by a lack of balance in yin and yang energies which flow through the body. Treatment methods are therefore needed to help a sick person harmonize these energies once again so that health may be restored.

The ancient Chinese art of acupuncture is an example of Taoist healing methodology. Acupuncture is now practiced, not only in China, but around the world. According to the principles of Taoism, ch'i flows freely through the body along certain pathways called meridians. The Taoists believe that blockages sometimes occur along these pathways, causing various illnesses. Acupuncture may be used to clear out these blockages so that the flow of ch'i may be facilitated once again. This is done by placing small needles into certain points along the body, known as acupuncture points. When these blocks are removed, the ch'i flows freely once again and the body heals itself.

In a book published by the Fetzer Foundation, entitled *Energy Fields in Medicine*, Brendan O'Regan wrote a chapter called "New Paradigms in Medicine: Can They Emerge?" In this chapter, he presents research which has been conducted on the practice of acupuncture. O'Regan points out how this form of healing has earned a legitimate place in the medical treatment of many illnesses. In another chapter of the same book, Yoshiakil Omura writes about Qi-Gong Therapy, which is another eastern method of healing. Qi Gong masters from China, by achieving certain states of mind which are balanced and centered, are able to treat patients with various illnesses and imbalances in their bodies. This process was illustrated in the Moyers' documentary when one patient described a feeling of centeredness and relaxation which eased her pain as she practiced moving the ch'i through her body under the guidance of a Qi Gong teacher.

Tai Chi Chuan

Tai Chi Chuan, often referred to simply as Tai Chi, is a meditative exercise based on the philosophy of Taoism. It is represented visually by the yin/yang symbol, dynamic and changing like the universe itself. In doing Tai Chi, one flows from the aspects of yin, which are considered to be *receptive*, to the aspects of yang, which are considered to be *expressive*. Moving back and forth between these two energies, the Tai Chi practitioner participates in a "dance of life," while allowing the breath to direct ch'i throughout the body. In the *I Ching,* an ancient Chinese text, it is stated that there are sixty-four ways to represent all the possible changes in the universe. These are pictorially represented by sixty-four hexagrams. For this reason, there are often sixty-four movements in the various forms of Tai Chi.

Tai Chi was apparently created when Chinese monks who wanted to gain the benefits of physical exercise while continuing to remain in a meditative state. They combined fighting techniques, taught in their own culture, with meditation techniques, taught by Buddhist teachers who had migrated to China from India. From these original exercises, Tai Chi and other martial arts apparently developed.

Tai Chi continues to be widely practiced in China today. It has also been introduced to other countries, including the United States, during the present century. Although there are many different forms of Tai Chi, all facilitate the integration of body, mind, and spirit. Some teachers emphasize the martial arts aspects and some do not. Many take lessons to lower their blood pressure or to better deal with the stresses in their lives. Students usually become more mentally alert, better able to concentrate, and more peaceful.

The steps in Tai Chi are patterned after the graceful movements of animals. One's breath is coordinated with each movement. Such names as "carry tiger to mountain," and "stork cools its wings," from the *Quong Ping* style of Tai Chi, refer to these movements. I learned the *Quong Ping* style through adult education classes. Because there were always new students coming into the class, our instructor would teach a beginning and an intermediate level during the same class, relying on her intermediate students to help the beginners. At a certain point, we would advance to the next class, which actually included both intermediate and advanced students. In that class, the advanced students would help the intermediate students. By helping each other, we were able to refine our skills even more. Because of the nature of the classes and my own schedule, it took me about two years to complete the entire form. It will take me the rest of my life to continue to refine the movements and to apply its principles.

There is always something new to be learned in practicing Tai Chi. Regardless of the form you may choose to study, all are graceful and meditative, helping you to integrate body, mind and spirit into your practice as well as into your daily life. In doing Tai Chi, one "flows like water" when the movements become automatic. Attention placed in each moment as it occurs allows the practitioner to be "in the flow," trusting that the future will unfold as it is meant to unfold.

Tai Chi teachers often stress the importance of allowing the breath to enter the body through the soles of the feet from deep within the earth itself. Allowing this breath to rise to the tan t'ien, an area just below the navel, it is then rotated by the waist and directed in different ways. After the energy is raised, it needs to then be grounded. This is why Tai Chi forms end with a grounding movement of some kind.

In his book, *Movements of Magic: The Spirit of Tai Chi Chuan*, Bob Klein uses the term "body-mind" to describe a kind of inner knowing which takes over when Tai Chi is being done in the most refined manner. When one relaxes into this kind of inner knowing, the conscious aspects of the mind connect to the subconscious aspects. At the same time, one is alert to being connected also to the outer environment. This allows the ch'i to flow through the body without any obstructions.

In attempting to teach others how to do the Tai Chi form, I find that I am unable to teach them by words alone. By doing the movements, however, I am able to demonstrate what needs to be done, guided by "body-mind" memories stored in my body.

Taoist Principles

During a particular time of meditation and receptivity to spirit communication, I became aware of inner guidance which was very Taoist in nature. I have presented the messages below for you in the form of principles which may be considered while walking the Taoist pathway. I have divided them into sections, according to the themes of the messages received.

Accept yourself as you are, while also remaining open to change for the better.

"Your journey consists of putting one foot in front of the other. You step with your left foot, empty your right foot. You fill your right foot and empty your left. When you stumble and fall, pick yourself up, brush yourself off, and start again, one step at a time, each time with greater awareness."

"Sense the energy which surrounds you. As you move through it, prepare yourself to move around obstacles without losing your balance. As in Tai Chi class, when you lose your step, look around for cues and support to get back in step. Remember, you are loved and supported in all that you do."

"You are too hard on yourself. Although you cannot go back and change your mistakes, you can avoid future errors by correcting your thinking. This way you avoid stumbling over the rocks in front of you. Soon there are fewer and fewer rocks to avoid and the path becomes more easily walked. Remember, you are in the light and you are not alone. Go in peace. Stay on the path."

This principle points out the importance of taking an honest look at ourselves in the context of our present life circumstances. It is important to realize that, even the most exciting journey always begins with the first step. By accepting ourselves as we are, we give ourselves the support and nurturance we need in order to make those changes we would like to make in our lives. Surely, we will make mistakes along the way, but that is often how we learn best. By acknowledging and correcting those mistakes, we are able to move to a new level in our understanding of how life works. It is also important to know that we sometimes need to reach out to others or to a power greater than ourselves in order to gain an understanding of what our next steps may be.

Live life from your center, and communicate with others from your center to theirs.

"You have learned some hard lessons. Now you must concentrate on becoming centered and balanced. Then you can take your center with you wherever you go. Communication and touching is not real unless it is from your center, reaching out to the center of the other, for that is where connection occurs. That is where the two are one."

"Reach out from your center, for that is who you are. If the other person reaches out from the center of who he is, you will connect in harmony. If not, the energy will go by without hurting you."

"There is an energy that is greater than your own which flows through you when you are centered and balanced. It is this energy with which we are interested, for it is the energy that is the most

powerful and the most worthwhile. This greater form of energy harmonizes, loves, plays, and heals."

This principle reminds us of the importance of approaching life from a balanced, centered position. In my own experience, I have learned that being centered is being in touch with my true essence. This enables me to be fully present in the situations in which I find myself. When I am centered, I am able to see clearly and objectively. When I am off center, my thinking is scattered and my perceptions are often clouded with emotional overtones. Sometimes we have to take time to regroup and center ourselves in order to see a situation clearly and objectively enough in order to deal with it effectively.

Don't forget to honor and respect yourself, as well as to honor and respect others, for the two are inseparable.

"You have an opportunity to be in touch with your body and to bring all of the parts into balance. Your body wants to be loved and you are learning to love, not only your body, but all of the qualities of your True Self as they are meant to be loved."

"Honor yourself as you honor others. Give yourself space as you respect the space of others. This means to respect every moment and every living thing you encounter. Life is honorable then and you, too, are honored by all who meet you."

"The best things in life are free, like the stars and the beauty of nature, an act of kindness, seeing within, and touching someone with love in the highest sense of the word."

This principle reminds us that we are not on this journey alone. Since we are constantly interacting with other people and other forms of life, it is important to have a healthy respect for our inter-relatedness. As we grow in our abilities to honor and respect ourselves, we do not need to seek recognition from others in order to feel complete. This frees us to interact with them in a more objective manner, honoring and respecting them as the individuals they are.

Practice concentration and focusing so that you can stay centered in yourself and in each moment as it presents itself to you.

"Merge with the universe a little, then bring your awareness back into focus for the next project. This is better than having half a mind on a given subject and half a mind on something else."

"Focus on your breath. Let it lead you to the farthest reaches of your mind. Let it also lead you to the depths of your mind. Let your attention become laser sharp and one-pointed. If you will do this, you will be able to see what you need to see and do in order to enhance your spiritual consciousness."

"Concentrate, focus, be clear. There is need for less physical activity and more right thinking. Practice Tai Chi. It will help you concentrate as you perform actions in the world, while also staying on your path."

By learning how to concentrate and focus our awareness, we improve our abilities to live life to the fullest. This is because the ability to concentrate and focus allows us to be fully present. The past does not exist anymore and the future is not yet here. The present moment is where life is happening and that is where we need to be if we are to fully live our lives.

Learn to relax. Trust the universe and let go of old patterns which no longer serve you.

"Releasing is part of receiving. When something new comes into our awareness it circulates and gets digested. If it doesn't fit, let it go. There's no way to hang on to old ideas when new learnings are coming in. It is the law of the universe."

"Relax and trust your knowing. You know more than you think you know. And don't forget to live your life. Be there in it. Don't just watch it go by or you will miss it completely."

"Relax all the muscles in your body, all the neurons in your brain. Any exercise you can do to relax is recommended. Trust the process of guidance. Know that you are being guided and all is unfolding as it should."

This principle reminds us that life is constantly changing and that we, too, are constantly changing and growing. In order to benefit from new understandings and insights which come our way, we must be willing to let go of those ideas which are no longer appropriate. Perhaps they served us at one time in our lives, but are now mere baggage, which needs to be released so that we may move more freely along our pathways.

Taoism is truly a path of beauty, simplicity, balance, and harmony. When practiced fully, it helps us to discover a place of peace within ourselves.

Concluding Comments

Some of the basic teachings from the Taoist way of life include the following:

All of creation originated in the Tao, which is the unifying principle holding all of life together.

The created universe is made up of yin and yang principles (feminine and masculine energies) which complement each other.

In order to live fully, it is important to be totally centered in the present, flowing gracefully into each new moment as it occurs.

In order for life energy (ch'i) to flow freely through our beings and bring us good health and long life, we need to keep our circuits (meridians) clear. There are techniques, such as Qi Gong, acupuncture, and Tai Chi Chuan, which help to facilitate this process.

According to Taoism, it is possible to learn how to direct the life energy (ch'i) which comes to us from the Tao.

Nature is a wonderful teacher. The cycles in nature are like the cycles in our lives.

We can expect life to constantly change. It is important to stay centered as we move through these changes gracefully.

Personal Reflections

I have personally experienced the teachings of Taoism through my practice of Tai Chi over the past fourteen years. In doing Tai Chi, I can calm my nerves, quiet my mind, and condition my body, all at one time. It is truly a dance with my Higher Self which transports me to another dimension, filled with peace, harmony, and beauty.

Sometimes, when practicing Tai Chi in a very meditative state, I see a light which shines out from my finger tips, providing me with a visual image of the energy which is flowing out from me. I am thus reminded that the Infinite Spirit is expressing through me in a very real way. In my Tai Chi classes and at other times when I am part of a group of people who are honoring the spiritual essence of life, I sometimes see a light emanating from others, as well as a light which surrounds us all with its radiance and warmth. This is very comforting to me and gives me a feeling of spiritual connection.

When I am really practicing Tai Chi the way it was meant to be practiced, I feel at harmony with myself and with all of creation. At times, when I forget my little self for a moment, I feel like "water flowing in a stream." As soon as my mind tries to label the experience, however, the feeling goes away. I am learning that sometimes it is better just to experience a "beingness," without trying to explain it or justify it with words. The more I practice, the more of these precious moments I have. Such a powerful practice cannot help but overflow into other aspects of life.

Practicing Tai Chi helps one to move through life with a greater sense of centeredness, grace and heightened awareness. It also helps to facilitate an understanding that nothing in life stays the same. Things are always changing in a cyclical manner, much like the seasons of the year. Times of good fortune naturally change to times of misfortune and then back to times of good fortune, much like one season changes to another in nature. In contemplating this, one is reminded of the old saying "This, too, shall pass." No matter how difficult a situation may be, it is comforting to know that, eventually, it will change. This has certainly been a comforting thought to me during some of the difficult times of my life.

I am also learning that, in order to be respected by others, I must first respect myself. As I learn to do this more and more, I am better able to know people as they really are, rather than thinking of them as "above" or "below" me. This opens a door to mutual respect and honest communication.

All too often, many of us tend to become overly involved with some aspects of our lives while neglecting other aspects which may be just as important. By making a few adjustments, however, we can achieve a greater sense of balance. Sometimes we have to let go of old patterns which no longer serve us in order to make room for new ways of being which are more conducive to positive growth. It is also important to remember that spiritual guidance is available to us as we face the challenges of our lives. As we learn to trust the universe and to let go of those old patterns which no longer serve us, we find that life unfolds more naturally.

Practice Exercises

Take a Tai-Chi Chuan class

Look at the schedule of classes from your local community college, adult education program, or park and recreation program. Many of them include Tai-Chi Chuan classes. There may also be a Tai-Chi Chuan studio in your community.

I Ching Readings

Try "consulting the oracle" in the ancient book of changes, called the *I Ching*. I like to use *I Ching* workbook by Robert Wing. While focusing on questions or concerns about your life, toss the coins or throw the sticks in the way described. Depending on how they fall, particular Chinese hexagrams are created. By looking up these hexagrams and reading the passages which are written about them, you may gain valuable insights into your life.

Meditations

Try the following meditations. They are similar to the ones my teacher, Patty O'Dea, used with our Tai Chi classes. First, record it on an audio cassette tape. Then listen to them while following the script.

#1 Sitting Meditation (designed to integrate body, mind, emotions, and spirit)

Sit in a chair that has a straight back with your feet touching the floor, legs uncrossed. Relax your shoulders and arms and place your hands softly on your lap with palms down. Lean back on the chair, with your spine straight. Imagine that your head is being held up by an invisible string of pearls, suspended from a star just above your head. Knowing that you are suspended in such a way allows you to relax your head, while also keeping your spine straight. Now allow the muscles in your face to relax and your eyes to softly close. Let go of any tension around your eyes so that they are just lightly closed as you sit here suspended from above. Allow your jaw muscles to relax and your tongue to gently touch the roof of your mouth, with lips slightly parted. Feel all the fine muscles of your face relaxing and gently letting go of any tightness. If you find your head nodding as you relax, allow the invisible string of pearls holding your head to gently draw it up again so that your spine remains in a straight line.

Now allow your neck and shoulders to let go of any tension they might have been holding. Relax your arms, hands, and fingers as they gently lay upon your lap. Relax your chest muscles and your back, feeling your organs inside relax as well. Now take a few minutes to allow this wonderful feeling of relaxation to extend to your upper and lower abdomen, your pelvic area, and finally down through your legs and feet.

In this wonderful place of complete relaxation, place your attention on your tan t'ien, an area which is about two inches below your navel. Breathe in gently, allowing your in-breath to fill your tan t'ien with soothing life energy. Now gently direct your out-breath up to your head, filling your brain with positive life energy. Allow any disruptive thoughts that come into your mind to gently fall away while you simply sit here in a totally relaxed state.

Now continue breathing in from the tan t'ien and gently direct your out-breath into your chest and heart, filling this area with wholesome life energy. Allow any disruptive emotions that you might have been holding in your heart to simply disappear as you sit here in total peace and harmony.

Now continue breathing in from the tan t'ien, gently directing your out-breath into the cells of your body, through your nerve pathways, and out to the tips of your fingers. Feel refreshing life energy fill your trunk, pelvic area, legs and toes.

And now, with your mind, emotions, and body harmonized and in balance, feel a flow of white light entering the top of your head from the star above you, filling your body, mind, and emotions with a sense of perfect health and spiritual well-being. Feel your entire being in balance and at peace.

And now, feel the chair beneath you and your back against the seat. Move your fingers and toes a little. Now rub your hands together. Remember to keep that inner sense of peace and harmony with you as you gently open your eyes and bring your awareness back to an outer focus.

#2 Tai Chi Walking (designed to harmonize body movements and breath)

Choose a room or outdoor area with a bit of space in front of you. Stand with your hands at your side, knees slightly bent, and head in alignment over your spine, as if a string of pearls, suspended from above, is holding it erect for you, without any effort on your part. Take some slow deep breaths and pay close attention to the air coming in and out of your nostrils as you inhale and exhale.

Inhale deeply. As you exhale, place all of your weight on your left foot. Keeping your weight on your left foot, begin to breathe in as you slowly roll your right heel up and gently lift your right foot off the ground, preparing to step forward. While keeping your weight on your left foot, gently place your right heel on the ground in front of you, beginning at the same time to exhale. Your out-breath coincides with a shift in weight to your right foot as you gently roll forward. Now keeping your weight on your right foot, breathe in as you slowly roll your left heel up and gently lift your left foot off the ground, preparing to step forward. While keeping your weight on your right foot, gently place your left heel on the ground in front of you, beginning at the same time to breathe out. Your out-breath coincides with a shift in weight to your left foot as you gently roll forward.

Continue stepping forward in this manner. Your in-breath coincides with the lifting of your foot and placing your heel forward. Your out-breath coincides with the shifting of weight to the other foot. Tai Chi walking is walking with concentrated awareness, designed to coordinate the breath, the movements of the body, and the shifting of weight as you move forward. It is indeed a metaphor for moving forward in life with concentrated awareness of each step you take along your pathway.

Now practice walking backward, continuing to coincide your in-breaths with lifting one foot and stepping backward, placing the toes down first before shifting weight to the back foot. As you breathe out, shift your weight onto the back foot. Breathe in again as you lift the forward foot and place your toes gently on the ground behind you. Breathe out as you again shift your weight. Walking backward in this manner helps you to test the ground behind you before shifting your weight. This helps you know if the way is clear of obstacles or dangers. This, too, is a metaphor for life. Test the ground carefully before stepping into unknown territory too quickly. Keep your balance as you move in different directions in the journey of your life.

Pamela Allen

Chapter Three
Hinduism

While traveling down the path of Hinduism, we encounter teachers, whose purpose it is to point to the Atman (Spirit) within us. As the Atman is awakened, we realize that we are spiritual beings, temporarily living in a physical world. This may be symbolized by the lotus blossom, which reveals its beauty above the water, while its roots reach down into the earth, connecting it to all of life.

Hinduism

Sacred Scriptures

The foundation for Hindu teachings comes from sacred scriptures, generally referred to as Vedic literature. Some of this material is believed to have been divinely revealed to ancient Hindu sages, who were known as Rishis. The Rishis transmitted what they had learned orally to their disciples, who then passed it down through the generations. At around 1000 years before the birth of Christ, the literature began to show up in written form. There are now four documents, known as *Vedas*, as well as a large number of documents known as *Upanishads*, which are believed to have been part of this early orally-transmitted material.

Another sacred text, believed to have been written by a human author, but based on early orally-transmitted teachings, is an epic known as the *Mahabbharata*. The famous *Bhagavad-Gita* (Song of the Lord) is part of this epic. Many refer to it simply as the *Gita*. In this epic, the deity, Krishna, is a charioteer for the great warrior, Arjuna. He uses a battlefield to teach Arjuna about fulfilling his sacred duty. His teachings include a description of the various kinds of yoga which are designed to be congruent with different kinds of personalities. They include: (1) Jnana Yoga (the way of wisdom), (2) Bhakti Yoga (the way of devotion), (3) Karma Yoga (the way of service), and (4) Raja Yoga (the way of meditation). Arjuna was advised to be true to his calling as other Hindus are also advised to do, the underlying philosophy being that each person's sacred duty is important and contributes to the well-being of the whole.

Other sacred writings, called *Sutras*, were written to describe practices within each of the Hindu Systems. Paramahansa Yogananda, in his famous book, *Autobiography of a Yogi*, writes about an authority on yoga by the name

44

of Patanjali, who is believed to have written the *Yoga Sutra* during the 2nd century B.C. The *Yoga Sutra* describes a yoga system known as the Eightfold Path. This path includes eight activities which are considered to be of utmost importance: good moral conduct, observance of religious principles, developing the right meditative posture, meditation, concentration, correct breathing (pranayama), the release of attachments, and super conscious states of consciousness (samadhi). Yogananda taught a form of Raja Yoga in a scientific manner, based on the Eightfold Path.

Historical Framework

Scholars (including Kim Knott, who wrote *Hinduism: A very Short Introduction*) suggest that this ancient religion dates back thousands of years before the birth of Christ. Some say it arose among the indigenous people in India, known as Dravidians. Others say it originated with a race of people known as Aryans, who migrated to India later. No one knows for sure when it first began, but most agree that it is probably one of the oldest religions on our planet. Hinduism continues to grow and expand into many areas of the world, taking on various forms depending on where it is practiced. It has also influenced the development of other religions, such as Buddhism and Sikhism.

According to Ed Viswanathan, who wrote *Am I a Hindu: The Hinduism Primer*, the word, Hindu, was originally used by the Persians who came to India in the sixth century. He suggests that many Indians would actually prefer to use the name, Sanathana Dharma (the eternal religion) rather than Hinduism. Hindu teachings are thought to have come from the eternal realms of Infinite Spirit (thus the reference to this pathway as an eternal religion).

45

Hinduism is not just a religion but is also a way of life for most of the people in India. For this reason, it's teachings are interwoven into societal attitudes. Though the philosophy of Hinduism is all-embracing and tolerant of many different belief systems, the caste system, which is a somewhat rigid system of categorizing people, still exists in India This system was modeled after the belief that one is born into a particular station in life because of past-life actions. Though there is some flexibility now, people in India generally stay within the caste into which they were born. This is because of the belief that they were born into the appropriate circumstances to fulfill the responsibilities they came to earth to fulfill.

There are four castes in India: (1) religious leaders, (2) administrators, (3) producers, such as farmers or artisans, and (4) those who provide services. Until "untouchability" was outlawed in 1950, there was also a fifth caste which was considered to contain the outcasts of society. These people were shunned by everyone else as being unclean. Many people, including Mahatma Ghandi, fought to change the concept of "untouchability" and helped to bring about needed legal reforms. Some Hindus, as well as western thinkers, are questioning whether it is time to revisit the caste system in India and to interpret the scriptures pertaining to it in a metaphorical, rather than literal sense.

Another controversial aspect of Indian society (especially from a western point of view) is the way in which women have been treated. This comes from an interpretation of the sacred scriptures which suggests that a woman's primary role in the society is to marry and take care of her husband's needs. Kim Knott *(Hinduism: A Very Short Introduction)* tells us that it wasn't until the latter part of the 20th century that women no longer had to present a dowry to their husbands in order to marry. Since the 1800's, Indian women have also had to fight for equal education.

There have been both western and Indian reformers, men and women alike, who have dedicated themselves to making changes for the betterment of women. Even though there have been many legal gains in terms of women's rights, there are still attitudinal changes which need to be addressed.

One of the most famous reformers in India, of course, was Mahatma Gandhi. Gandhi helped to improve attitudes toward women and the lower castes but is probably best known for his use of non-violence in order to help bring about India's independence from England in 1947. Martin Luther King Jr., in the 1960's, used the same non-violent philosophy in fighting for the civil rights of African Americans.

The Role of Gurus

The sacred teachings of Hinduism are brought to the people by spiritual leaders known as gurus. One of the ways to become a guru is to be a male born into the brahmin caste (the caste for religious leaders) and to study the sacred scriptures in one of the monasteries. Those who are good at sharing this knowledge with others may become gurus, who travel around as teachers. Some of the teachers choose to go back to the monasteries to perform the sacred rituals associated with the practice of Hinduism. Their roles would then be similar to those of a priest in Christianity or rabbi in Judaism.

There is another method for becoming a guru, which is open to both men and women as well as to members of all of the different castes. Those who experience Self Realization through individual meditative practices, regardless of their knowledge of the *Vedas* or their level of formal education, are encouraged to teach others. Indeed the essence of most forms of Hinduism is that of realizing that there is divinity within oneself, known as the Atman, which may be realized through meditative practices. Having realized the Atman, gurus have the authority to assist others in making the same discovery.

It is refreshing to know that women in India, as well as men, have been allowed to become spiritual teachers. Knott (*Hinduism: A Very Short Introduction*) discusses one such example. She was Anandamayi Ma, who lived and taught during the 1800's. This teacher demonstrated such motherly qualities that she became known as Ma, which means "mother." She is said to have experienced the Atman directly as a result of her individual meditations.

A more modern female guru, who is also revered for her motherly qualities, is Mata Amritanandamayi. After achieving Self Realization, she was inspirational to many disciples. In order to review some of her teachings, I would suggest that you read *For my Children: Spiritual Teachings of Mata Amritanandamayi*.

Many people from around the world come to the monastic communities in India or to the Hindu organizations in other countries, looking for gurus to teach them the way to Self Realization. These spiritual teachers help their disciples or devotees to release physical attachments so that spiritual truths may reveal themselves more easily. They also point to the "truth teacher" or "sat guru" which may only be contacted within the core of each person's own being.

Western Expansion of Hinduism

Let us now look at some of the spiritual teachers or gurus from India who have brought the Hindu philosophy to western countries. One such teacher was Vivekananda, who brought the teachings of the Advaita Vedanta System to the west. This system is a non-dualistic interpretation of some of the teachings found in the *Upanishads*. (In India, there is also a Dvaita (dualistic) Vedanta System which highlights the difference between God and human beings and stresses the need for devotion in approaching God.) Both the non-dualistic and dualistic approaches have been acceptable within Hinduism as legitimate pathways to God. The Advaita Vedanta System, however, has been more popular in the west.

A more contemporary guru, Sri Chimnoy, has been influential in the 20th century in spreading some of the ideas originally brought by Vivekananda. He is also known for the beautiful music he has written for the flute and for using that music as a medium to deepen meditative practices.

Another well known guru from the 20th century is Paramahansa Yogananda. Following the instructions of his guru, he brought the ancient teachings of Kriya Yoga to America. Yogananda is well known for the book, *Autobiography of a Yogi,* in which he gives westerners a real look into the lives of some of the famous yogis and saints in India. He also presents information regarding the Kriya Yoga path, which is one of the most advanced forms of yoga in existence today. Yogananda established the Self Realization Fellowship in the United States, which includes several temples in California, as well as retreat centers and monastic communities where spiritual seekers may go for instruction.

Some of the other 20th century gurus who have become well-known include Swami Muktananda, Bhagwan Rajneesh (also known as Osho), and Sathya Sai Baba. Muktananda promoted the teachings of Siddha Yoga to people all over the world. Osho is known for promoting the philosophy of Tantra Yoga. Sathya Sai Baba, who is still living, is said to be able to use the power of his mind in order to materialize matter from spiritual realms. Many devotees of Sai Baba claim to feel his presence when they meditate, even though they are physically far away from him. Sai Baba is considered by his followers to be an Avatar, or incarnation of the manifestation of God known as Vishnu.

There have also been western teachers who have facilitated the growth of Hinduism in the world. One such teacher was Annie Besant, who went to live in India in the late 1800's. She had previously studied theosophy, which blends some of the teachings of Hinduism and Buddhism with occult teachings. While living in India, Besant promoted Hinduism in the face of the criticism being levied by the Christian missionaries.

Another more contemporary spiritual teacher is American-born Gangaji, who studied meditation in India with her guru, Sri H.W.L. Poonjaji. Poonjaji had been a disciple of a very famous guru and Indian saint, Sri Ramana Maharshi. On her audio tape, entitled *Who Are You: The Path of Self Inquiry*, Gangaji explains how her guru helped to stop the thoughts in her mind so that she could realize the truth of her being. Upon her Self Realization, she was instructed by him to become a spiritual teacher in the west. Gangaji followed his instructions and came back to the United States where she holds regular seminars, referred to as satsang. These are sessions in which she meditates with her students and answers their questions. Like the Indian gurus before her, Gangaji points her followers to the "sat guru" or truth teacher within themselves.

Another American teacher of ancient Hindu principles in the 1980's's was Russell Schofield, who founded the School of Actualism. His book, *Joyous Exploration*, was written in poetic form and is filled with beautiful photographs showing various meditative poses. Schofield's center in Escondido, CA was considered by many to be a modern mystery school, helping to bring awareness to students of the union with God to be found within oneself.

Basic Teachings

Divine Oneness, Expressed Through Multiplicity

One of the most important teachings in Hinduism is the quality of Divine Oneness. This is a concept which is taught in many spiritual pathways. Though it may seem that Hindus worship many gods and goddesses, these deities actually represent the many manifestations of the One Divine God, which exists in every aspect of the universe, including human beings.

Within Hinduism, the One God is sometimes referred to in an abstract manner such as Infinite Spirit and, at other times, more personally such as Divine Mother. Likewise, different aspects of God may be worshipped. These aspects are represented by the various gods and goddesses within the religion. Of the many aspects of God mentioned in the literature, there appear to be three primary ones, the Creator (known as Brahma, with his female counterpart, Saraswati), the Preserver (known as Vishnu, with his female counterpart, Parvati), and the Destroyer or Dissolver (known as Shiva, with his counterpart, Shakti). The sound, AUM (pronounced "ohm"), is thought to contain the vibrations representative of these three aspects of God. By chanting the AUM, it is suggested that one may connect with God's energy.

The gods, Brahma, Vishnu, and Shiva represent the out-flowing energy of God whereas the goddesses, Saraswati, Parvati, and Shakti represent the in-flowing energy. I like to think of the masculine energy as God's out-breath and the feminine energy as God's in-breath.

Realization of the Divine Within

Within the philosophy of Hinduism, it is taught that God dwells within human beings in the form of the Atman. This is like that which has been called the Higher Self in other cultures. When the Atman or Higher Self is fully realized, one is said to be Self Realized. Another teaching within Hinduism is that the Law of Karma (Cause and Effect) exists in the created universe. According to this system, people experience the effects of their actions. Hindus believe that people experience karma even from previous lifetimes and that they live, die, and experience rebirth into the circumstances in life which reflect the karma they have accumulated. As they become more and more evolved, their actions eventually lead to a life-time in which Self Realization is possible. Once this is achieved, it is believed that souls do not need to continue in the cycle of birth and rebirth without any consciousness of why this is happening. They may, instead, choose to experience life in a non-physical realm or to come back to the physical world in order to assist others in the process of liberation or Self Realization.

In addition to the Law of Karma, Hinduism also teaches that there are three qualities (referred to as gunas) which interact in one's life during their evolution toward Self Realization. These include a desire to keep things the same (tamas), a desire to change things (rajas), and a desire to return to God (sattva). The more one clings to physical experiences, the more the quality of tamas is influential. The more one is willing to change, the more the quality of rajas plays a part. The more one desires to unite with God, the more the quality of sattva predominates.

When one begins to realize that the physical realm is merely a veil of illusion (Maya) and that it is the Divine Within (Atman) which is permanent and eternal, then it is possible for Self Realization to occur. After awakening to the truth of one's being, one must still go about the business of living in a physical environment. The difference, however, is that this is done with conscious awareness of what is real and what is illusory.

The Chakra System

Hinduism teaches a form of energy exchange known as the Chakra System. Understanding this system helps to provide a foundation for the yoga practices which are taught as practical applications of Hinduism. Chakra is actually a Sanskrit word which means "wheel." The chakra system is made up of "wheels of energy" which are considered to be aligned in a particular way along the spine of a human being. The chakras operate at an electrical frequency which the body can withstand. Through these energy stations, information from non-physical realms can be sent to physical beings and vice versa. Caroline Myss, in her book, *Anatomy of the Spirit*, describes chakras as being like little computers, processing information in a way that we, the users, can understand it.

There are said to be seven major chakras in the body and another above the head. Although these chakras are invisible to ordinary vision, those who are considered to be clairvoyant are often able to see them with "psychic eyes." Each chakra processes a certain kind of information and is seen as having a different color. I have chosen to present the colors suggested by Neil Cohen in his chart, *Chakra Awareness Guide,* in the descriptions which follow.

The root or base chakra is located at the base of the spine. It is said to have slower vibrations than the ones above it. The color often associated with the root chakra is red. It stands for one's connection to the physical realm. The energy activated in it helps one to survive in this earthly realm. Since physical matter is dense, this chakra must vibrate at a slower pace so that in-coming electrical impulses may be understood at this level. The sense of smell and the element of earth are associated with the root chakra. People whose root chakras are blocked may have difficulty realizing that there are other aspects to life besides physical survival. When the root chakra is awakened, however, one feels grounded and ready for higher levels of experience to be manifested.

The second chakra is found around the area of the navel and is generally referred to as the navel chakra. The color usually associated with it is orange and the sense it activates is taste. The navel chakra vibrates at a little faster speed than the root chakra and is related to issues of sexuality, creativity, relationships, finances, and the process of change. Though this chakra still vibrates within physical density, it is the one which receives information to help people establish relationships outside of themselves.

The solar plexus chakra is the third one, located just above the navel. Its color is yellow, like fire. This is considered to be the center of personal power and self esteem. Fire is the element associated with the solar plexus chakra as well as the sense of sight. Issues related to the energy activated in this chakra include one's sense of confidence and individuality as well as the ability to be assertive in the physical world. If this chakra is blocked, it might be very difficult for a person to take risks.

The fourth, or heart chakra, is located near the center of the chest and is associated with the color, green, and the sense of touch. The element of air is represented here. This chakra and the ones above it vibrate faster than the three physical chakras below them. This is because they process information which relates to emotions, thoughts, and insights. The heart chakra is where one's emotions become activated and where one learns compassion, peace, harmony, openness, and love.

The throat, or fifth chakra, is represented by the light blue color of the sky. Ether is the element and hearing is the sense associated with this chakra. Communication originates here as well as one's intention or will. It is the area which becomes affected when the struggle between honoring one's own intentions or the intentions of others is at stake. The highest form of awakening at this chakra, paradoxically, involves the ability to release the personal will, by choice, to a higher power or God.

The sixth center is the so-called "third eye" or brow chakra. Its color is indigo. This chakra is considered to be the seat of wisdom, clairvoyance, and guidance. It is the center which is located in the forehead between the eyebrows. The element is light. Blockages here may cause one to have headaches and difficulty concentrating because this chakra deals with mental issues. This is where insight, imagination, and the ability to concentrate are derived.

The crown chakra is sometimes described as a thousand-petaled lotus. It is located on the top of the head. When the lower energies are awakened and balanced, they are said to be raised to this region, where cosmic consciousness is possible. This is where enlightenment is possible for it is where union with the Divine takes place. Like a lotus which grows above the water with it's roots below in the mud, this chakra symbolizes our lives, rooted in the physical, but also united with the higher realms of truth.

As one engages in spiritual practices, such as chanting, meditation, singing the names of God, or just in living one's life, electrical energy goes in and out of the chakras. If any of them is blocked, not enough energy can come in or go out. This may result in illness, fatigue, or depression. In order to feel vibrantly alive, one needs to keep the chakras open and awake. This allows the energy needed in life to keep circulating effectively. Some of the yoga pathways which help to assist in the opening and activation of the various chakras within the body are described below.

Yoga Pathways

Yoga, in Sanskrit, means "yoke" or "union" and refers to union with the Atman, or Divine Within. Like the Vedanta discussed earlier, yoga is a system within Hinduism which may serve as the focus of one's spiritual practice. There are many different kinds of yoga which may be practiced for this purpose. For the purposes of this chapter, I have chosen to highlight some of the better-known ones which are practiced in the west, as well as in India.

Hatha Yoga

Hatha Yoga is one of the best known forms of yoga practiced in the world today. In fact it is what most people in the west think of whenever they hear the word, yoga. It is a form of physical exercise which includes a number of postures (asanas) designed to bring harmony to the masculine and feminine energies in the body, sometimes referred to as sun and moon energies. These asanas help to awaken and align the chakras in such as way that life energy (prana) may flow freely through them, thus enlivening the body, mind, and spirit. The asanas also help to stretch our muscles and joints as well as to improve the functioning of our glands. In addition, the practice of this form of yoga helps to develop positive attitudes and good health which lead to longevity.

The philosophy behind Hatha Yoga is that one's breath is closely associated with the body and mind. Working with the breath while practicing the various postures helps to condition the body so that it can utilize other forms of meditation in which breath-work is very important.

In most Hatha Yoga classes, some form of inner meditation is practiced in addition to the breath-work, stretching exercises, and postures. For example at the beginning of each class, participants are generally instructed to sit or lie quietly and still their minds. Then again at the end of each session, participants are often guided in a meditation while they rest quietly with minds and bodies still.

Kriya Yoga

We have already touched upon Kriya Yoga as the form of yoga brought to the west by Paramahansa Yogananda. It is a very advanced form of Raja Yoga which focuses on breath-work (pranayama). Prana refers to vital energy, and yama refers to regulation of the breath. By practicing this form of yoga, one learns to slow down the functions of the heart and lungs so that increasingly higher levels of consciousness, and eventually cosmic consciousness, may be experienced.

Because this is such an advanced form of yoga, it is important to have a guru or spiritual teacher in order to guide one in the practice of Kriya Yoga. It is suggested by the Self Realization Fellowship that one take the introductory correspondence classes for approximately a year before being initiated into the more formal aspects of Kriya Yoga (which need the assistance of a guru or spiritual teacher).

Mantra Yoga

Mantra Yoga uses sacred sounds and phrases in order to still the mind and focus on the Divine. A mantra is a system of sounds which are produced at certain frequencies in order to facilitate meditation. Transcendental Meditation (TM) is probably one of the best known forms of Mantra Yoga. In TM, the teacher assigns mantras which are individualized to suit each particular student. This mantra is to be repeated over and over during a session in the morning as well as during a session in the evening. Transcendental Meditation has been very successful in working with people without an extensive background in Hinduism.

There are many mantras which may be used to practice this type of yoga. For instance, the repetition of the various names of God or other phrases may be used to bring one's attention to the Divine. The sound, AUM, is said to include the three frequencies of God and, in fact, to include

57

all the frequencies in the universe. It is believed by many that, by chanting AUM, one may experience union with the Divine.

Tantra Yoga

Tantra Yoga is different from the other yogas in that it focuses on living fully within the physical world rather than attempting to transcend it. In doing so, one brings a sacred awareness to all of life. In Tantra Yoga, sexual energy is seen as being representative of the play between the masculine or absolute aspect of God (Shiva) and the feminine or creative aspect of God (Shakti). When the two combine, it is like a marriage of spiritual and physical energies. In his book, *Tantra Spirituality and Sex*, Osho suggests that the sex act when viewed in this manner, may be considered sacred.

Another aspect of Tantra Yoga is called the rising of the kundalini. Lee Sannella, in his book, *The Kundalini Experience: Psychosis or Transcendence*, describes the kundalini as being a power, located in the base chakra, curled up, so to speak, like a serpent. When the "serpent" awakens, it then rises up through the body's various chakra points until it reaches the crown chakra. This enables one to experience cosmic consciousness.

Sometimes a spontaneous awakening of the kundalini occurs before the person has meditated enough to strengthen the physical body for this experience. This may result in physical or emotional pain and confusion. For this reason, it is extremely important to have a teacher or guru to assist one in meditative practices designed to help make this a positive experience.

Siddha Yoga

As mentioned earlier, Swami Muktananda brought Siddha Yoga to many parts of the world. The SYDA Foundation continues to further his work. When one has experienced an awakening of his or her divine nature, spiritual gifts and abilities (siddhis) often become developed. These gifts may include such paranormal abilities as clairvoyance or mental telepathy. The purpose of Siddha Yoga, however, is not to develop these abilities even though they may come as a by-product of spiritual awakening. The most important goal is to realize the divine nature of oneself. Aspects of Siddha Yoga include chanting, devotional singing, and meditation.

Agni Yoga (Actualism)

As mentioned earlier, Agni Yoga was utilized by Russell Schofield in the 1980's, in order to teach the principles of what he called Actualism. Actualism refers to the process of becoming actualized or awakened to the Divine Within. It utilizes fire or light energy (symbolized by the manifestation of God, known as Agni) to cleanse, purify, and heal the body in order to facilitate this awakening. This is done through various exercises in which colored lights are visualized while focusing on certain areas of the body. It is important to have a teacher to guide one through these exercises because they may bring out powerful emotions. Actualism has been considered to be one of the modern-day mystery schools of the west, teaching methods of healing which actually have their roots in the Hinduism of India.

Concluding Comments

Hinduism appears to be a very rich and multifaceted spiritual pathway. There are systems within systems which may be studied or practiced if one desires to do so. We have focused our attention on just two of these systems, the Vedanta and Yoga Pathways. There is a wealth of information on the Internet and in your references which may be used for more in-depth study.

In the philosophy of Hinduism, there appear to be some key points which stand out. For example, most Hindus believe the following:

There is an Infinite Spirit, or God, which permeates all of existence.

The Infinite Spirit manifests itself in a multitude of ways, both masculine and feminine, and may be worshipped in a multitude of ways.

A veil of illusion pervades the physical universe. As human beings become too attached to these illusions, they forget that they are basically spiritual in nature.

There is a system of energy exchange between physical bodies and the non-physical realms of existence. This is called the Chakra System. As one awakens the chakras, one conditions the body so that higher truths may manifest through them.

There are many spiritual teachers and sacred texts which point to the truth of who one is. In addition, there are yoga techniques (including asanas or postures, breathing exercises, mantras, visualization techniques, and meditations) which help to unite the body with that which is Divine.

A goal of Hinduism is to awaken to the realization of the Divine Within, known as the Atman.

When seekers finally awaken to the truth of who they are, the veil of illusion is pierced and the soul becomes liberated.

Personal Reflections

Although I have some difficulty accepting the rationale for the caste system in India, I do appreciate the philosophical foundations within Hinduism. For example, I like the fact that Hinduism honors all religions as legitimate pathways to God. Even within its own traditions, Hinduism allows room for various interpretations of the truth.

I have had the pleasure of experiencing various aspects of Hinduism over the past several years, beginning with classes in Actualism (Agni Yoga) in the late 1980's and continuing with metaphysical classes at a Spiritualist Church in Encinitas, CA in the 1990's. Even though the latter classes were in Spiritualism, the curriculum included instruction in the Hindu Chakra System.

Although I did not have the privilege of meeting Yogananda while he was in physical form, I have enjoyed visiting the beautiful garden at the Self Realization Fellowship retreat center in Encinitas, CA. I have also visited two of the Self Realization temples for Sunday services. I found it interesting that a portrait of Jesus was hanging in the front of these temples, along with Yogananda and his lineage of gurus. In the Self Realization Fellowship, Jesus is considered to be a master teacher like some of the gurus of India. As mentioned before, Hinduism does not separate itself from other religions but, in a sense, embraces all pathways which lead to God.

One of the synchronistic events which occurred when I started to write this chapter was my sister's decision to send me three books which she had been given on Hindu thought. They had been given to her by an old friend who happened to be a student of a spiritual teacher by the name of Eugene Davis. Upon receiving the books, I was very pleasantly surprised to find out that Davis is actually a direct disciple of Paramahansa Yogananda. His books enriched my studies of Yogananda's teachings and are included in the reference section at the end of the book.

I have also had the privilege of being in the presence of three of the gurus mentioned in this chapter: Swami Muktananda, Sri Chimnoy, and Gangaji. A very good friend of mine was a devotee of Muktananda and invited me to attend a wedding he was performing in Santa Monica, CA (for numerous couples who wanted to be married in the traditional Hindu manner by their guru). It was very beautiful to behold and I could sense the immense spiritual power emanating from Muktananda.

I met Sri Chimnoy with my daughter, Kerry, who had heard of him while attending classes at San Diego State University. After attending a workshop given by some of his devotees, we traveled to Los Angeles to see Sri Chimnoy in person in the LA airport where he spoke to a group of devotees there. Expecting him to be dressed in traditional Hindu garb, I was surprised to see him wearing a contemporary jogging suit. As it turned out, he is a physical fitness advocate and teaches that exercise, as well as meditation, is very good for the soul.

Another spiritual teacher to whom I have been exposed is Gangaji. I attended two of her seminars in the San Diego area and was quite impressed with her presence as well as her messages. I find Gangaji to be a clear and beautiful light in the world and look forward to spending more quality time in her presence.

My present connection to Hindu thought is through a Hatha Yoga class, taught by a very good friend of mine, Barbara (Ayosea) Morse. I can already feel the positive results of my participation in this wonderful class. Others I know, who take Hatha Yoga, also speak of how beneficial it is to them.

Practice Exercises

The following meditation is one which I like to use in the morning before I get up and face the day. I actually sit up in bed to do it but you may also sit in a chair or on the floor. You may want to tape the following instructions and play the tape as you sit quietly and experience this meditation. After you have become familiar with the procedure, you will probably choose to do it without the tape. This way you will be able to stay at each chakra as long as you like, without hurrying through the exercise. I like to dwell, for example, on the brow chakra, or third eye, until my mind has been stilled. Then I may ask for spiritual guidance.

Wherever you choose to sit, make sure that your back is straight. If you sit on the floor, cross your legs in an easy position or in a half lotus or lotus position. You may use a pillow, with your knees forward, if that is more comfortable. In the half lotus position, your left foot rests on your right thigh or your right foot on your left thigh. In the full lotus position, your right foot rests on your left thigh and your left foot rests on your right thigh. Hands may be on your knees, palms up, with thumb and forefingers touching to make little circles. Another position would be to place one hand under the other, palms up, with thumbs lightly touching.

Instructions:

Close your eyes or soften your gaze and imagine your first chakra at the base of your spine. Visualize the color, red. Think about how secure you feel in your surroundings. Feel your connection with Mother Earth and the sense of a strong foundation in the physical world.

Now move your awareness to the second chakra, just below your navel. This chakra is orange. Feel the energy of this creative chakra as you breathe in and out

63

from this area in your body. Know that your relationships are positive and that you are attracting just the right people and resources into your life.

Now let your awareness rise to your solar plexus, just above your navel. Visualize the color, yellow. Feel this chakra as your "inner sun," making you strong and self confident. Feel the warmth here and bask in a sense of well being.

Now move your awareness to your fourth chakra, the area of your heart. Imagine the color, green as you feel warmth, love and compassion in your heart chakra. Know inside your heart of hearts that you are very much loved and have an endless supply of love to give to others.

Now move your awareness to the throat area. Imagine a sky-blue color here as you focus on your intentions in life. What is it that you most want? Are you living according to your highest intention for yourself or are you allowing someone else's will to disempower you? Now imagine that you release your will to a Higher Source. See how peaceful this makes you feel, how protected and loved.

Now let your awareness move to your brow chakra, the area of your third eye. See the color, indigo and feel your mind relax and open to receive intuitive wisdom. Relax into a feeling of clarity and insight. You may want to come back here at a later time to ask for guidance in your life.

Now let your awareness rise to your crown chakra on the top of your head. Visualize a beautiful lavender color which flows all around you, enveloping you in peace and beauty and light. All is well as you sit here enjoying the life energy which is gathered here.

Now imagine a white waterfall of light flowing in from above your head through your crown chakra and down through each of the other ones... brow, throat, heart, solar plexus, navel, and root. Now imagine all of your chakras to be cleansed, bright, and awake, ready to bring you all of the positive energy you need to live a beautiful and meaningful life. When you are ready, slowly move your fingers and toes a little, bringing your awareness back to the physical space where you began this meditation. Then gradually open your eyes and feel energized, harmonized, and very much at peace within yourself.

Let us end this chapter with a word which is often used to end yoga classes and other spiritual gatherings. It means "The light, or divine, in me greets the light, or divine in you."

Namaste!

Pamela Allen

Chapter Four
Buddhism

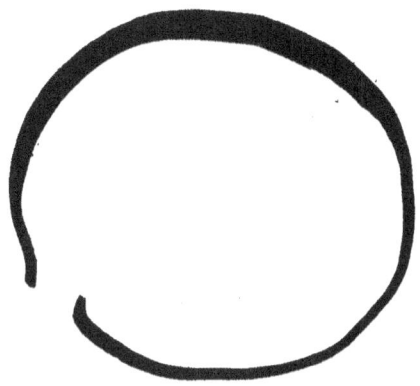

As we travel down the path of Buddhism, we learn the art of living in the present moment, in touch with the center of ourselves, while experiencing life on the outside with greater presence and simplicity. Buddha not only listened to the Spirit Within, but was fully awakened to It. This path teaches us to recognize our connection with all other beings and to develop hearts of compassion.

Buddhism

Introduction

Traveling along the Buddhist pathway may be described as traveling through life with heightened awareness of each moment as it presents itself. By being fully present in life as it unfolds, one may learn to be part of everything that occurs. By not dwelling on past events (which no longer exist) or dreaming of future events (which may never come to pass), one is free to be in the here and now, as it is occurring, inseparable from it, and fully alive. This is the gift which Buddhism brings to those who practice this way of being in the world.

There are various forms of Buddhism being practiced today, including Mahayana, Theravada, Zen, and others. Though these forms have developed in different cultures around the world, all may be traced back to the original teachings of Siddhartha Gautama, who was born a prince in an Indian kingdom during the sixth century, B.C.

Siddhartha Gautama grew up in a palace with all of the earthly goods he could ever have wanted. He eventually married and had a son. Although he could have stayed with his family for the rest of his days, Gautama felt that he must leave the palace gates in order to go out into the world to gain a broader perspective of what life was about. In India, it was considered acceptable for a person of Gautama's status to choose this kind of lifestyle if he so desired.

In his travels, Gautama witnessed the suffering of those who were old, sick, or dying. He also saw a wandering spiritual ascetic, who seemed to have a sense of peace about him. Wanting to know how this person could find peace and happiness amidst the inevitable suffering in life, Gautama decided to become a wandering ascetic himself.

Gautama felt that he needed a teacher who could answer the questions in his heart and mind. Unsuccessful in his mission, he finally gave up the search and simply sat down in meditation, determined to stay there until he became enlightened. After many, many days of meditating, without food or drink, under a tree which became known as the famous Bodhi Tree, Gautama finally received the answers he was seeking and obtained enlightenment. He became known as Shakyamuni Buddha, which means "the awakened one." Buddhism developed as a result of his teachings. This new spiritual pathway eventually spread from India to other parts of the world, including Tibet, Southeast Asia, China, and Japan. More recently, Buddhism has been introduced to people in Europe and America.

It is important to note that the Buddha's teachings were incongruent with the authoritarian rules of the caste system being practiced in India at that time. With this new teaching, people who were born into poor circumstances and status in life suddenly had hope that they could improve their lot in life. Buddha taught the benefits of following a middle path between excessive privilege and poverty.

According to Steve Hagen, who wrote *Buddhism: Plain and Simple*, Buddha began to teach four important truths. The first is that suffering is an aspect of life. The second is that suffering is caused by greed and excessive desires. The third is that greed and excessive desires may be released in order to change one's suffering. This involves changing one's thinking patterns as well as actions. The fourth truth is known as The Eightfold Path (not to be confused with the Eightfold Path in Yoga described in the last chapter). The Eightfold Path in Buddhism includes (1) seeing the world as it truly is, in accordance with the first three truths mentioned above, (2) having an intention to live according to those truths, (3) speaking, (4) acting, and (5) seeking a livelihood in accordance with those truths, (6) putting forth the right amount of effort in one's activities, (7) being mindful, and (8) meditating on a regular basis.

With his enlightenment, the Buddha became free from attachments. He no longer experienced desire for the material things in life. He knew that he was part of everything in the universe. With this awareness, he developed a heart of compassion for all living things. His followers sought to follow his example.

The Importance of Compassion

The importance of compassion, in order to eliminate suffering in the world, is a central tenet of Buddhism. A compassionate person has concern for others and, in a sense, feels their pain. Buddha taught that each individual who develops a heart of compassion affects all other individuals in the world. This occurs because individuals originate from a common life force. If it is true that all beings are interconnected, it follows logically that all beings are negatively affected if one suffers, and that all are positively affected if one shows compassion. According to this line of reasoning, compassion may be seen as essential in order to eliminate the suffering which exists in the world.

In developing a heart of compassion, it is important, according to the Buddhist belief system, to let go of the ego (false perception of the self). When the ego is released, a more universal, authentic Self may be realized. This Self is part of all that is, with no separations or boundaries.

The Dalai Lama, Tibetan spiritual leader, was forced to leave Tibet when the Chinese government invaded his country. He is an individual who exemplifies compassion in his every-day life and in his teachings. In his book, *The Power of Compassion*, he states that he feels compassion, rather than anger, for the Chinese government, even though they forced him into exile.

Buddha taught that the life force, from which all beings originate, never dies and continues to express itself in many forms. Rebirth occurs in the sense that future lives are shaped by present experiences. According to this system of thought, people who practice compassionate living in today's world may actually help to bring about a more compassionate world in the future.

Jack Kornfield wrote a book entitled, *A Path With Heart,* in which he addresses the subject of compassion. By learning to love others and show compassion for them, he suggests, one learns to live in a heart-felt way. This, he believes, gives meaning and beauty to life. In order to love others and to be compassionate toward them, Kornfield and others suggest that human beings must first learn to love and demonstrate compassion for themselves. Some exercises for developing a heart of compassion may be found in Kornfield's book.

Most people who practice Buddhism strive to speak and behave in ways which will promote the quality of compassion in their daily lives. They try to have livelihoods which are congruent with this ideal and strive to use their energy wisely so that their efforts may be sustained. In addition, they pay attention to the thoughts which they have during their daily lives, using meditation as a tool to develop greater focus and concentration. Mindful living, they feel, will enable them to experience life more fully and authentically. Since meditation and mindfulness are important aspects of the Buddhist pathway, they are each explored further in the next two sections.

Meditation

It is important to note that, according to the Buddhist system of thought, individuals may discover universal truths by quieting their minds and entering a place of stillness through the process of meditation. What is practiced in meditative sessions must then be consciously integrated into daily activities in order for negative thought patterns to be released and authentic living patterns to be developed. Even though a teacher is important along the way, that teacher should not be placed on a pedestal. The student is considered to be equal to the teacher in terms of potential for enlightenment. The importance of recognizing the equality between teacher and student is emphasized by Sheldon Kopp in his book, *If You Meet the Guru on the Road, Kill Him.*

It is said that Gautama became an enlightened being through the practice of meditation. By quieting his mind, he was able to become receptive to inner wisdom. This inner wisdom taught him that he was part of everything around him, rather than just a physical body, separated from other physical bodies. By feeling his connection to a greater, more universal Self, Buddha was able to let go of his feelings of attachment to transient, earthly things which had previously served to enhance his ego (false belief system of himself as a limited, physical being).

In order to gain some first-hand experience with meditation, it is suggested that you try practicing zazen, a meditation technique stemming from Zen Buddhism. The directions for doing zazen are presented in the Practice Exercises of this chapter. As mentioned earlier, Zen originated in Japan and has since spread to the United States, where many Zen centers and monasteries have been created. Zazen may be used to quiet the mind of its constant chatter so that a direct experience of life may be appreciated. This direct experience is much like the kind of life children enjoy naturally before their minds are cluttered with society's expectations. It is a state of mind in which one feels the essence of pure innocence and beingness.

One of the most practical guides for practicing zazen is a book by Shunru Suzuki, entitled *Zen Mind, Beginner's Mind*. Suzuki teaches his students to sit quietly, concentrating on the breath as it moves in and out of the nostrils until a state of peace is attained. Wandering, random thoughts or feelings will usually come up during this time. They are simply acknowledged and released. As the mind calms during the meditation process, it may be likened to that of a lake, which begins with many ripples and gradually becomes calm and serene. If the moon were shining on such a lake, its reflection would be clearly seen. Likewise, a calm and serene mind will more accurately reflect life's situations than a mind which is busy and distracted. This is one of the reasons for practicing zazen or any other form of meditation.

As part of their teaching techniques, some Zen masters give their students paradoxical puzzles, called koans, to solve. The idea of the koan is to exhaust the rational mind so that the student may become receptive to intuitive and spiritual insights. An example of one of the more famous koans is "What is your original face, before your parents were born?" In other words, who are you really, beyond the flesh and bones which make up your body? To answer such an illogical question, the student must exhaust all logical attempts and surrender to a spiritual truth which is beyond logic. This comes after deep meditation concerning the koan, along with assistance from one's teacher. Solving such a koan may free one to new ways of understanding the meaning of life.

Meditation helps us to develop the quality of mindfulness, or heightened awareness, of each moment as it presents itself during the course of each day. This is important if we are to recognize and release false identities so that more compassionate, authentic ways of living may be developed.

Mindfulness

Mindfulness may be described as being present and aware of each moment as it presents itself during the course of one's daily activities. In the Buddhist tradition, it is felt that being mindful in this way connects one to a form of inner wisdom. By having an open mind, one is better able to observe what is happening in the moment, rather than prejudging what is about to happen.

Thich Nhat Hanh, in his book, *The Miracle of Mindfulness,* discusses how to incorporate mindfulness into one's daily activities. For example, when doing one's chores, it is important to concentrate on the chores rather than on the next activity one will be doing. Buddhists stress the importance of being fully present, no matter what the project may be. They further suggest that it is helpful to practice a complete "day of mindfulness" from time to time.

While practicing mindfulness, various mantras (self statements) may be said in silence as one goes about daily activities. For example, one may think, "I am now arising into a new day" or "I am now eating bread." By being in a state of mindfulness, one does not miss out on life as it is passing by. Every activity may be viewed as a sacred event, worthy of full attention, even those experiences which are painful.

Wisdom is achieved, according to the Buddhist thought system, when one is able to see reality as being perfect as it is, without the need for additions or subtractions. From this standpoint, it is important to be in a state of mindfulness even when approaching death or experiencing the death of a loved one. The Tibetan Buddhists have even written a manual on death, called *The Tibetan Book of the Dead*. In this manual, procedures are presented for assisting a dying person in making a smooth transition to the spirit side of life.

By practicing mindfulness, one has the opportunity to study the self and to release false, judgmental ways of being in the world so that more objective, authentic living patterns may be developed. By releasing false ways of being in the world, one practices the quality of non-attachment. If a feeling of sadness comes up, for example, one may simply think "I am feeling sad about so and so." By looking at the feeling in an objective way and then releasing it, one may avoid falling deeper and deeper into a depression. In this way, one takes hold of the mind rather than letting the thoughts of the mind take hold of oneself.

Mindfulness helps to reconnect us with life so that stressors may be dealt with in an effective way. When we live with deep awareness of our connection to all of life, the Buddhists say that it is possible to experience a state of mind which is like having heaven, or nirvana, on earth.

Concluding Comments

Some of the key teachings in Buddhism are as follows:

All beings are interconnected. When one suffers, all suffer. When one is compassionate, all benefit.

When one achieves an empty mind, it is possible to feel union with all beings. This facilitates the development of compassion.

When one lets go of ego attachments (false perceptions), it is possible for the Authentic Self to emerge.

Being compassionate to other beings begins with being compassionate to oneself.

Mindfulness and meditation help one to live in the present moment.

Wisdom is seeing reality as it truly is, without adding or subtracting from it.

Heaven (Nirvana) is the blissful state of mind in which one feels connected to all that is, without any sense of separation.

Personal Reflections

In my own life, Zen has played an important part in my spiritual development. I was brought up in the Protestant Christian tradition, but found that I needed something more inner directed in order to be fulfilled spiritually. After moving from Florida to California in 1974, I was given the opportunity to explore meditation as a tool for directing my attention inward. I joined a group which met in the home of a Zen teacher on a weekly basis. We practiced zazen, walked in a meditative fashion, and listened to Zen scriptures. We did some chanting and drank tea together, in stillness and with mindfulness. This provided a community for me in which to develop my Zen practice. I kept journal notes during the period of time I was involved in this group. I also used poetry as a vehicle for expressing some of the wondrous sensations associated with meditation practices.

Looking back at my journal notes, I am reminded of how mindful I was during meditation of physical feelings and pains in my body, as well as thoughts about various attachments in my life. Sounds and smells also became part of my awareness. In some group sessions, incense was burned. Sometimes soft music played while we filed into the hall. Then the music stopped and a gong was sounded. I followed the sound of the gong to the very end of its vibration. Then, when two sticks were hit together, the meditation session began and there was silence in the room.

The practice of zazen has helped me to quiet my mind. Even if this occurs for only a minute or two, it is worth the effort. When one's mind is still, it is possible to have that wonderful feeling of connection with all that is, without any need to change anything. This is a very blissful state of being. Of course it is difficult to maintain such a state, but it is nice to know that it is possible.

In my meditation practice, I have learned to notice whatever emerges and then to release my attention to it. For example, I sometimes notice colors surrounding the meditation area or on the wall. I try not to become too fascinated by this, but rather to merely note it and continue meditating.

In addition to the pleasant sensations which sometimes accompany meditation, there may also be negative, or painful sensations. Sometimes I notice pains in my body or feelings of sadness which arise in my consciousness. Whatever the feeling is, I have learned that it will eventually fade away if I simply recognize it and do not attach too much importance to it.

In order to benefit from practicing meditation, it is important to set aside time to do it on a regular basis. One of the ways I learned to facilitate my commitment to meditate was to start with a timer and a commitment to sit only for five minutes at a time. Gradually it became easier for me to increase the time. I found myself not wanting to stop when the timer would go off. This was a cue that it was time to extend the practice period.

In the group meditations I have attended, chanting has often been an integral part of the experience. I find that the sound of the chanting usually takes on the sound of one voice, ancient and strange, yet very beautiful and comforting. Interestingly, this sensation is similar to what I have felt while singing Native American songs.

While drinking tea or eating in a meditation group setting, it is customary to bow to the one serving. This is a sign of respect and gratitude.

Listening to the chewing of food and being aware of the taste of the hot tea are all part of the practice of developing mindfulness. In this way, drinking and eating practices are not taken for granted. I find that everything is enhanced by this silent awareness.

The more I practice meditation in daily life, the more serene and centered I feel and the better my life flows. This is also true when I have to deal with very painful or difficult situations. For instance, when my mother died recently, I was with her in the hospital at the moment she left her physical body. She opened her eyes and looked at each of us in the room as if to say good-bye. The morning sun was streaming in the window, causing her face to glow. I knew at that moment that her death was a very essential and natural part of her life. I felt privileged to be present at this important time and comforted in the feeling of connection to her. This feeling of connection was just as strong when she died as it had been when she was alive. Buddhism helps me to understand the strong feeling of connection which I have with my mother, as well as with others in my life, and, indeed, with all of creation. That is truly a beautiful gift.

Practice Exercises

The following suggested exercises will give you a personal experience of some of the practical ways to use Buddhist practices on your spiritual pathway.

Practice Zazen (A Zen Buddhist Sitting Meditation)

Choose a quiet place for your meditation session. You may want to burn incense and/or hit a gong before you begin your practice sessions. Place your pillow or chair facing a blank wall. If you prefer to sit on the floor, it will help to use a small round pillow. You may want to buy a zafu (a meditation pillow) for this purpose. Any very firm, small pillow will work. I like to put a mat under my pillow. You may sit in a full lotus, half lotus, or relaxed position. By sitting on the edge of the pillow, your knees will be on the floor, to help balance your body. In a full lotus position, the right foot is placed on the left thigh and the left foot is placed on the right thigh. In the half lotus position, only one foot is placed on the thigh of the other leg. In the relaxed position, the legs are crossed in a comfortable manner. You may choose, alternatively, to sit in a chair.

Keep your spine straight, as if your head is holding up the ceiling. Your hands are held in what is called a mudra position (right palm under left palm, both palms up, and thumbs barely touching each other, creating an oval shape). The back of your right hand barely touches your lap. Elbows are held out from your body, as if cradling your hands. Keep your tongue on the roof of your mouth. Keep your eyes half open and somewhat lowered, your gaze about two or three feet ahead on the floor or the bottom part of the wall.

On the inhale, your lower abdomen, known as the hara, is filled with air. On the exhale, this area is emptied of air. Begin by inhaling. Then, on the exhale, silently think of the number "one." On the next inhale, silently think of the number "two." This is followed by an exhale, silently counted as "three." The process continues until the number "ten" is reached and then begins all over again. This silent counting of breaths continues until your mind becomes very quiet and still.

When your mind is still, you may choose to stop the counting process and just sit in the silence. If your attention wanders, the counting may begin again. This is done until the session ends. A session may vary from a few minutes to over an hour, depending on the level at which you are practicing.

The idea is simply to observe your feelings or thoughts, rather than allowing them to take your attention away from meditation. Do not attempt to stuff them down or deny their presence. Neither allow them to escalate and intensify. Simply observe them and watch them fade away. You are practicing mindfulness, presence, and one-pointedness.

Instead of counting breaths, you could also think such thoughts as "I am breathing in peace. I am breathing out love." Use whatever positive affirmations you choose.

It helps to have a community of like-minded people to support one's meditative practices. In Zen Buddhism, this community is referred to as sangha. The teachings of Buddha are called the dharma. Zen centers are usually headed by a master teacher referred to as a roshi. A roshi not only teaches with words, but also by example.

Zen masters are generally spontaneous and able to be fully present to the needs of their students and available for those teachable moments which present themselves. They also tend to use humor to teach students what patterns of behavior they need to give up in order to enjoy their lives more fully. True Zen masters also have hearts of compassion and are available to help their students to move beyond the barriers and challenges which present themselves during their practice.

When you are ready, you may want to go to a retreat for more than one day. Personal interviews with the roshi, or teacher, are available during this time so that you may ask questions or obtain instruction as needed.

Practice Mindfulness

Choose a day to practice being silent and mindful of each event that takes place throughout the day. If your attention wanders from focusing on the event of the moment, give yourself an inner message, such as, "I am eating this orange." Remember, when eating, really notice the taste and texture of the food. When drinking, really notice how the beverage feels as you swallow it. Take note of emotions which come up as well. Then simply let them go. Be open to the next event which is about to occur. After your day has come to an end, you may want to record some notes in your journal, which may be used to enhance your awareness of yourself. Sometimes there are groups which practice mindfulness together. Be on the look-out for such groups. Another idea is to take a walk out in nature and practice the art of being mindful and totally present.

Use Affirmations

Tibetan Buddhist teachers suggest that affirmations are helpful in developing certain qualities. For example, you might use the following affirmation: While gazing at a friend or even a stranger, say to yourself, "I see the Buddha in your face."

In Jack Kornfield's book, *A Path With Heart*, there are meditations, based on the Theravada Buddhist tradition, which he calls "insight meditations." In some of these, he offers affirmations which may be repeated to enhance the development of higher qualities, such as loving-kindness, peace, and centeredness. Try some of them. Kornfield also suggests ways of using meditation to deal with difficulties and to promote healing in one's life.

Chapter Five
Kabbalah

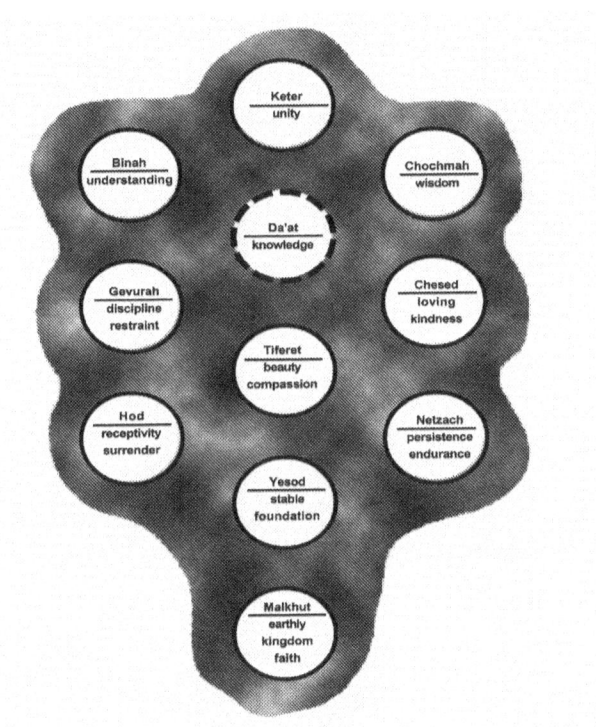

As we travel down the path of Kabbalah, we recognize our connection to all of life and to our creator. As we journey back to our Divine Source, the Tree of Life assists us in balancing out the polar aspects of our natures. As we reconnect with our own divine essence, we are invited to assist the creator in bringing forth divine qualities (such as love, joy, peace, and beauty) to the physical world in which we live.

Kabbalah

Overview

The Kabbalah is an ancient mystical tradition within Judaism. It is a mysterious pathway which was hidden for many years. According to *Encarta: World English Dictionary*, Kabbalah is sometimes spelled "cabala" and means "a body of mystical Jewish teachings based on an interpretation of hidden meanings in the Hebrew Scriptures." It also refers to "a set of secret or mystical beliefs" coming ultimately from the Hebrew word "qabbalah" which means "tradition," and "qibbel" which means "to receive, accept." It is also described as "something received or handed down." Kabbalist teachings about the workings of the universe were originally handed down by word of mouth to Jewish males who were considered to be mature and stable enough to handle the material. Over time many of the oral teachings were written down and eventually became available for study by both men and women, Jews and non-Jews.

Some Christian writers have made associations of their faith with the Kabbalah. Although these will be mentioned, the majority of the material in this chapter will be presented from the Jewish perspective because the roots of Kabbalah are in Judaism. Though it may be more difficult for those without a Jewish background to fully understand how the Kabbalah is interwoven with the teachings of the Torah and other Jewish texts, there is still much for all to learn from studying this mystical pathway.

If you are like me, it may take some time for the teachings of the Kabbalah to make sense to you. My suggestion is to simply relax your mind as much as possible as you make your way down this mystical pathway, enjoying the beautiful metaphorical imagery along the way. You may find, as I have, that the symbols become more real and alive for you as you allow them to play around in your mind over time.

Historical Framework

Scholars suggest that the roots of Kabbalah may go back to something referred to as Merkabah mysticism. This is a form of mysticism which is discussed in the Biblical book of Ezekiel. Merkabah means "chariot" and refers to a chariot of fire in which Ezekiel envisioned the prophet, Elijah, rising up to heaven. It also symbolically represents the soul's ascent into union with the Divine. This ascent is the soul's mission, according to Kabbalist teachings.

Rabbi Aryeh Kaplan, who wrote a book called *Inner Space: Introduction to Kabbalah, Meditation and Prophecy,* tells us that, according to Jewish faith, Moses orally received the Torah (first five books of the Bible) from God and passed its wisdom down to Joshua, who then passed it down to the prophets and elders among the Israelites. Kaplan explains that Moses was receptive to the art of prophecy and was able to transmit this art to Joshua. In a Kabbalistic sense, the art of prophecy refers to the ability to receive wisdom and guidance from the Divine. The early Kabbalists studied the secrets of Merkabah mysticism, obscurely embedded in the book of Ezekiel and other orally transmitted wisdom, in order to become receptive to this art of prophecy.

Early Jewish mystical teachings have sometimes been compared with the Gnostic movement prevalent during the first and second centuries. Gnosticism was a movement which included both Jews and early Christians. Like the Kabbalists, Gnostics believed that human beings could have a direct relationship with the Divine. Jesus Christ taught this and was an example of it as well. David Sheinkin, in his book, *Path of the Kabbalah,* suggests that, because of the similarity of his teachings with Kabbalist ideas, Jesus may have been exposed to this mystical wisdom prior to his ministry.

The early Gnostics were attacked by the orthodox Christians who believed that they were heretics. In the same way, the Jewish mystics were attacked by the orthodox rabbis. Concerned that the mystical ideas in the Book of Ezekiel were dangerous, they wanted the Jews to focus on following the Laws of Moses rather than delving into mystical meditative practices. However, Jewish mystics continued to read Ezekiel and to practice mysticism in secret.

Rabbi Aryeh Kaplan recently translated and wrote commentaries on one of the earliest Kabbalist texts, entitled *Sefer Yetzirah: The Book of Creation.* Some say that the original book was an oral one, taught by Abraham and later by Rabbi Akiva, who lived during the first century. Rabbi Akiva was a master of Merkabah mysticism and passed down his teachings orally to his students. Many of his students took notes, which were passed down as well. Eventually the *Sefer Yetzirah* was published around the 11th or 12th century. Kaplan's translation and commentaries contain numerical and astrological information, as well as details regarding the importance of the Hebrew alphabet, which Kabbalists believe contain hidden wisdom regarding the process utilized in the creation of the universe. Many of Rabbi Akiva's teachings, along with those of his student, Rabbi Simeon bar Yohai and others, were compiled in a book entitled, *Pirke Avot*, which means "the sayings of the fathers." Scholars say that this book was probably not written down until around the third century, though the sayings were from a much earlier time. If you are interested in reading some of the wise and beautiful passages from this period in Judaic history, there are two references at the end of this chapter, one by Rabbi Shapiro and one edited by Kravitz and Olitzky.

Rabbi Akiva's student, Rabbi Simeon bar Yohai, is thought to have been responsible for orally transmitting the material which was later published in another famous Kabbalist text, entitled *Zohar: Book of Splendor* (referred to in this chapter simply as the *Zohar*). In order to guard the secrets of Kabbalist teachings, metaphors were used in the *Zohar* to obscure its meaning. The *Zohar* is said to have been published during the 13th century by the Spanish Kabbalist, Moses de Leon. Many scholars credit De Leon with writing the book, though De Leon claimed that it came from Rabbi Simeon. Some say that De Leon was merely trying to give the book more credence by such a claim. Others say that he may have channeled Rabbi Simeon, using a process known as automatic or inspirational writing. In spite of the controversy surrounding it, the *Zohar* has stood the test of time and is now widely considered to be one of the most important literary works within the Path of Kabbalah. You may want to read Gershom Scholem's book, *Zohar, the Book of Splendor: Basic Readings from the Kabbalah,* to get a flavor of the literary richness of the *Zohar*.

Another early Kabbalist teacher was Abraham Abulafia, who lived during the 13th century and was influenced by Sufi teachings about meditation. He developed a system of meditation in which the combinations of Hebrew letters and names were chanted in certain ways in order to receive prophetic messages from the realms of the Divine. One of his students, Joseph Gikatilla, was known for his work on the Sefirot (manifestations of the Divine) depicted in the Tree of Life illustrated at the beginning of this chapter. We will discuss the Tree of Life more thoroughly later on.

By the 16th century, many Kabbalist thinkers had settled in Israel, in a city called Safed. Two of the important teachers during this time were Moses Cordovera and his student, Isaac Luria. Luria is known for his contributions to the Kabbalists' understanding of the creation process.

Known as the Ari, or lion, Luria refined the material according to insights he obtained through meditation. He was widely considered to be a mystical prophet in the Kabbalist movement.

During the 1700's and 1800's, Kabbalist teachings overlapped somewhat with the development of Hasidism, another mystical branch of Judaism which began in eastern Europe under the influence of Rabbi Israel ben Eliezer, who became known as the Baal-Shem. Martin Buber, in his book, *The Legend of the Baal-Shem,* tells us that Baal-Shem means "master of God's name." The Baal-Shem and other leaders in the movement were known as the tzaddik, or holy men. They taught primarily through stories and metaphors.

Hasidism, as a movement, was different from the Kabbalist movement in that it was taught to the uneducated villagers rather than being reserved for the elite few. The Hasids were influenced by Sufism, a mystical movement within Islam, as well as by Gnosticism, a mystical branch of Christianity. These two pathways will be discussed in the sixth and seventh chapters, respectively. Hasidism still exists, but not in the vital form that it did in the early days. Kabbalist teachings, on the other hand, have experienced a renewal in modern times, as they have been made available to everyone. Both Kabbalists and Hasids longed for a mystical communion with God and emphasized this in their teachings and practices. They also talked about the importance of viewing the ordinary events of daily life as sacred in nature. In viewing life this way, they suggested that human beings may elevate their lives from the physical realm to the spiritual realm and, by doing so, commune with God.

Kabbalist authors in the 20th and 21st centuries bring many different aspects of the pathway to light, based on their individual interests and expertise. Some of them are listed for you in the reference section. As mentioned earlier, Areyeh Kaplan translated the *Sefer Yetzirah* and also wrote *Inner Space: Introduction to Kabbalah, Meditation, and Prophecy*, which is an excellent reference on the Jewish Tree of Life. Another author, Gershom Scholem, has done a translation of the *Zohar* and is considered to be a leading Kabbalist historian. Rabbi David Cooper has contributed useful information about the meditative aspects of Kabbalah. He has also suggested that many Kabbalist practices overlap with the meditations found in such spiritual systems as Taoism, Buddhism, Hinduism, and Sufism. Other authors, such as Sheldon Kramer and Z'ev ben Shimon Halevi, have focused on the psychological applications of Kabbalah to everyday life. There is much to be learned as one travels down the Kabbalist pathway, with all of its twists and turns. Please see the reference section of this chapter for these and other authors' contributions which may be helpful in your own journey.

The Kabbalist Story of Creation

Many Kabbalist teachings are based on the creation process as described in the *Sefir Yetzirah* and the *Zohar*. I first heard about this process in a story told by my Kabbalah teacher and friend, Maura Richman. It is presented below in my own words, based on Maura's telling of the story, as well as data from other sources which I have discovered.

In the beginning, there was a vast sea of nothingness and from that nothingness issued forth a beautiful and endless light, a light so bright that it filled everything that was. This light was a reflection of that which is infinite, without end, non-dualistic, and about which nothing could be said.

For whatever reason, there arose within Ein Sof an intention to create something which would appear to be separate from itself. In order to make this happen, Ein Sof withdrew its light from the center out, forming a vacuum within

89

which the creation would take place. This process is known in Hebrew as tzimtzun, which means withdrawal or contraction.

After contracting and withdrawing its light, Ein Sof sent out a thin ray of light into the space which had been vacated. At the end of the ray of light, which emanated from Ein Sof, were five dimensions or universes. These dimensions included Ein Sof's will to create, undifferentiated mind, differentiated thought, speech, and action. As each new dimension of creation developed, the light encompassing it became dimmer and dimmer. When the last dimension was created, Ein Sof's light was dim enough for physical forms to appear to be separate. Had Ein Sof's light continued to be as bright as it was before the creation process, these forms, which make up our present physical universe, would not have been visible at all. This is why it seems that we are each separate from Ein Sof and from each other, but, according to the teachings of the Kabbalah, we are all part of Ein Sof's light.

Kabbalists tell us that divine emanations known as Sefirot make up the DNA of all of creation, including that of human beings. The Sefirot have been described as the faces or attributes of Ein Sof. They have also been described as the divine channels through which Ein Sof's light flows out to those of us in the physical universe and through which our light flows back to Ein Sof. The Sefirot make up the Kabbalist Tree of Life.

Some say that Ein Sof created vessels to contain the light of the Sefirot. The first three Sefirot were created perfectly and the vessels held together very well. The next seven, however, were unable to hold the light of Ein Sof and shattered, scattering Ein Sof's light in all directions. Some of the light returned to Ein Sof and some fell into the material universe, becoming trapped, along with the broken shards of vessels, in what appeared to be husks or shells

Most of us have been wounded by events in our lives. These wounds show up in emotions such as fear, doubt, sadness, and anger. As we recognize the sparks of divinity from Ein Sof within us, we also recognize the potential for healing ourselves and others. As we consciously work together with our loved ones to heal ourselves and our planet, we are symbolically raising our sparks of divinity back to the heavenly realms from which they came. By considering every aspect of life to be sacred in nature, we bring divine assistance into our lives. The Kabbalists say that, when all of Ein Sof's sparks have been returned, the Messiah will come and usher in a time of peace and harmony on our planet.

According to Kabbalist teachings, we human beings were created from Ein Sof, but have been given free will to live our lives as far away from it's light as we desire. We are symbolically keeping our divine sparks hidden if we do this. By the same token, we may choose to draw closer to Ein Sof's divine light by way of our intention, thoughts, and actions. This has been referred to as "raising the sparks" of our divinity. The Hasids use the term, *tikkun,* to describe this process of freeing the sparks of Ein Sof's light from the husks which have kept them hidden and thus, repairing our souls.

As our souls evolve, according to Kabbalist teachings, we tend to choose a movement toward Ein Sof's light. By doing so, we align with Ein Sof in order to assist in the co-creation of life. Rabbi David Cooper describes this process as "God-ing."

The Tree of Life

The Tree of Life is an ancient symbol which has been a part of other spiritual pathways as well as the Path of Kabbalah. The way it is used by Kabbalists, however, is especially unique and practical. Illustrated at the beginning of this chapter, the Kabbalist Tree of Life depicts the manifestations of a higher power, source of divinity, or supreme being, which many people in the western world refer to as God. In addition, it is said to express the substance (DNA) out of which the universe, including all of humanity, was originally created. The Sefirot, which make up the various aspects of the Tree of Life, are often described as the underlying forces of creation (spiritual, mental, emotional, and physical). They are said to influence us, while we, in turn, influence them. Indeed, this is how the co-creation process supposedly works.

The Kabbalists believe that spiritual and physical actions are connected. By balancing out the qualities of the Tree of Life in our own lives, according to this philosophy, we may actually affect the universe as a whole. This co-creation process is viewed as a joint venture between Ein Sof and those human beings who are aligned with It for the purpose of bringing about a more harmonious world.

The Sefirot, which are depicted in the Kabbalist Tree of Life, are thought to be reflected in all of creation, including the human soul. Please note the illustration of The Tree of Life at the beginning of this chapter as we go through a description of each of the Sefirot and how they work together.

The Upper Sefirot (Keter, Chochmah, Binah, and Da'at)

Keter is represented by the circle at the top of the Tree of Life. It is described as being made of pure, undifferentiated spiritual energy, coming from the nothingness of Ein Sof. During the creation process, Keter was (and still remains) united with Ein Sof, while also expressing Its intention to create something separate. Keter is described as being the will of Ein Sof to create humanity.

The quality of our souls associated with Keter is *unity*, a feeling of oneness with our creator. If we think of Keter in relation to our bodies, it is something like a crown of light above our heads, serving as a reminder that we are still connected to our source even though we cannot explain this in words. Keter also represents that feeling of inspiration (spirit within us) which moves us to create something meaningful out of our lives.

Like Keter, Chochmah (pictured on the top right column of the Tree of Life) is very close to Ein Sof. It represents the quality of *wisdom* contained within the undifferentiated aspect of our minds. Though Chochmah may not be known in a logical sense, it contains the expansive energy and inspiration needed for creation to take place. Chochmah has been described as the Divine Father of all creation. It is like the seed of something before it is actually manifested in the physical world.

I have recognized the intuitive guidance of Chochmah in my own life as that still, small voice within me which often nudges me in a certain direction when I am faced with an important decision. When I have listened to the voice and heeded its message, the results have usually been positive. When I have disregarded the voice and acted in a different manner, I have often had negative consequences to pay.

As Chochmah is at the top of the right column of the Tree of Life, Binah is at the top of the left column. It was the next Sefirah to emanate after Chochmah. Binah is like the Divine Mother of all of creation, the one which holds the expansive energy of the Divine Father. Binah represents the beginning of something which arises out of nothing. It may also be described as differentiated thought, associated with the quality of *understanding.*

Da'at (depicted with a dotted line around it in the Tree of Life) is considered to be the hidden Sefirah. It is like the glue which holds things together even when we human beings do not realize this. When revealed, it connects the intuitive wisdom of Chochmah with the rational understanding of Binah. In some ways Da'at is like *gnosis,* or inner knowing. (We will discuss *gnosis* more thoroughly in the next chapter.) Literature on the Tree of Life seems to infer that Da'at and Keter are like two sides of the same coin. Keter is that sense of *unity,* which is felt, whereas Da'at is that sense of *knowledge,* which can be thought about. Together, they represent the paradox of being united with all that is while also knowing oneself in differentiated form. This is somewhat similar to the teachings of Taoism, which we discussed in Chapter Two.

The upper Sefirot represent the realms of spirit and mind in that they describe the manner in which intuition and rational thought are held in balance by the quality of unity. Likewise, Da'at, Chochmah, and Binah represent the revealing of spiritual and mental truths in the form of knowledge. In the human realm, this may be associated with the right and left sides of our brains, unified by higher spiritual processes which, when allowed to work cooperatively in an integrated fashion, reveal true knowledge. The goal of integrating these various energies, according to my Kabbalist teacher, Maura Richman, is to "understand with wisdom and to be wise with understanding." Another way of saying this is "to have a thoughtful mind and mindful thought" as true knowledge reveals itself to us.

The Triad of Chesed, Gevurah, and Tiferet

Chesed represents loving-kindness, unrestrained and expansive. It is the quality of life which makes it possible for us to give of ourselves unconditionally to other human beings as well as to those activities which we enjoy. Love is the single-most important quality in life for it gives nurturance and meaning to everything else.

Gevurah represents discipline and restraint, allowing us to set limits. Parents must say "no" to their children sometimes, in order to teach them safe and effective ways to move about in the world. If parents never say "no," their children do not learn how to protect themselves.

In a romantic relationship, Gevurah is necessary so that one mate does not smother the other with so many expressions of love that there is no space or time for the other to respond. Gevurah is also needed in the process of creation. For example, an artist needs discipline, as well as love, in order to create something of beauty.

That which is formed by a combination of love and discipline is Tiferet, which represents *beauty* and *compassion*. It is represented in our hearts, for that is where we experience our most profound feelings. If people always receive love without any discipline, they may grow up expecting everything to be given to them all of the time. Discipline and restraint added to that love, however, gives them a chance to take responsibility for shaping that which has been given. Likewise, in order to be compassionate, one needs to have experienced both love and restraint. Otherwise it would be difficult to empathize with others who are suffering. Tiferet is considered to be that place of beauty and harmony, sitting at the heart or center of the Tree of Life, where all the other Sefirot are synthesized.

Whereas the upper Sefirot represent the realms of spirit and mind, the triad of Chesed, Gevurah, and Tiferet represents the realm of emotions. It is here that Tiferet (beauty and compassion) harmonizes the qualities of Gevurah (discipline and restraint) with those of Chesed (loving-kindness). Without the limiting nature of Gevurah, Chesed would continue to expand and create, without stopping. By the same token, discipline and restraint, without loving-kindness, would be very unpleasant indeed. When Gevurah is out of balance, it may even cause that which appears to be evil to take place on earth. Chesed and Gevurah become unified in Tiferet, where the qualities of love and discipline are harmonized in order to bring about beauty and compassion in the world.

The Triad of Netzach, Hod, and Yesod

Netzach represents *persistence* and *endurance*. It takes determination to go the distance to achieve victory. A person with a good sense of Netzach can stand up for his or her beliefs and do what it takes to realize ambitions.

One might refer to an Olympic athlete as a good example of a person with this kind of quality in his or her personality. On the other hand, too much Netzach may lead to too much willfulness to reach one's goals at the expense of other important aspects of life. For example, a person may be so involved in creating success in the work place that family and creative pursuits are ignored. Too much Netzach may also lead to addictions which are difficult to release.

Hod represents the qualities of *receptivity* and *surrender*. Sometimes it is important to stop moving forward in life and become receptive to the opportunities which show up unexpectedly. The receptive person is able to learn as well as teach, and to receive as well as give. The splendor and majesty of a sunset is only available to the person who stops long enough to take it in.

Albert Einstein demonstrated the importance of becoming receptive. After working very hard on his projects, he would be sure to take breaks and relax, often turning to music to assist in this process. It was during those times of relaxation when insights would often come to him, to help solve the problems with which he had been struggling. Many of us have had the experience of trying to solve a problem and being unable to do so. When we just "sleep on it" for a night, the answer to the problem often comes the next day. This is an example of becoming receptive.

Like receptivity, surrender is also an important aspect of Hod. Sometimes it is important to surrender one's personal will so that a greater good may be demonstrated in the world. Hod lets us know when it is time to stop what we are doing in order to surrender our will to a divine source which knows the fuller picture better than we do.

Yesod represents a *stable foundation*, from which one may act in a responsible manner in the world. Yesod symbolizes the ability to stand in the center of our being, while maintaining a calm attitude even in the midst of turmoil. It speaks to the ability to handle crises which come in life, without falling apart. It is in Yesod where we establish roots in life which are strong and dependable. This comes from a combination of working to achieve our goals, while also being receptive to opportunities which come to us for free. Yesod also represents the ability to maintain our individual identities while surrendering our egos to possibilities which lie beyond our own abilities. Some people would call this "surrendering to a higher power."

In summary, Netzach, Hod, and Yesod represent the realm of *emotions in action*. Netzach enables us to set goals and to work hard to achieve them. Hod enables us to receive the gifts of life. Yesod, representing stability, unifies the qualities of hard work and receptivity in order to assist us in creating a firm, stable foundation, which will not fall apart during difficult times.

In Judaism, the union of Netzach and Hod is sometimes personified on earth by the sexual union between a husband and wife who wish to bring something spiritual (represented by their marriage) into the world. The man's creative energy is received by the woman and often-times results in the birth of children who continue to carry forth the united qualities of their parents, plus many of their own, into the physical world. Both giving and receiving are necessary qualities for the foundation of the family to be established.

The Lowest Sefirot (Malkhut)

All of the prior Sefirot channel their energy through Yesod to the lowest Sefirah, Malkhut. The term, Malkhut, represents the *earthly kingdom* within which we live. Malkhut is that place where spiritual and physical elements come together. Another quality of Malkhut is that of *faith*. (It takes faith for a person in the physical world to believe that it is possible to connect with that which is Divine.)

Malkhut is sometimes referred to as the Shekhinah (the feminine aspect of God, underlying all of creation). The masculine aspect of God, on the other hand, is that which did the creating. Since the Shekhinah dwells within nature, it is also referred to as the divine nature of God which exists in all things. This is similar to the Native American description of Mother Earth. The Hasids speak of the Shekhinah as being united with that which has been created on earth. They teach that, by honoring her, we may learn to recognize the presence of the spiritual realm within the physical realm of nature.

Malkhut/Shekhinah is the doorway through which the Kabbalist travels in ascending the Tree of Life. In this way, human beings bring physical reality to Ein Sof's purposes. When a person has faith that it is actually possible to unify with the Divine, he or she is ready to climb the Tree of Life.

The Three Columns of the Tree of Life

Another way to look at the Tree of Life is to consider the three columns which make it up. The right column represents expansion. It is considered to be masculine in nature, headed by Chochmah (sometimes referred to as the Divine Father). Chochmah represents wisdom which is still undifferentiated from Ein Sof's light. Below Chochmah is Chesed, representing loving-kindness, which is out-pouring in nature. Below Chesed is Netzach, representing persistence and endurance. The energy of Netzach is expansive, moving forward to accomplish goals and achieve victory. Wisdom and loving-kindness help to fuel Netzach's pursuit of meaningful goals in life.

The column on the left represents restraint. It is feminine in nature, headed by Binah (sometimes described as the Divine Mother). Binah provides a container, so to speak, for the wisdom of Chochmah to be transformed into differentiated thought forms which are capable of being understood. Below Binah is Gevurah, which represents restraint and discipline. As one learns to hold back in Gevurah, one is assisted in becoming receptive enough to surrender to the Divine in Hod (located below Gevurah in the left column).

The middle column of integration represents the most direct line of connection to Ein Sof. Beginning with Malkhut, we learn to have faith that there is a connection between the spiritual and physical realms of life. In Yesod, we develop a strong and stable foundation by harmonizing the expansive and restraining manifestations of the Sefirot on the right and left columns. In Tiferet, we develop the capacity to experience beauty and compassion so that we may wisely integrate Ein Sof's loving intention for our lives. It is there in Tiferet that we begin to experience our connection to Ein Sof. Finally, in Keter, we experience ourselves as being unified with Ein Sof and at one with all that is. When this has been achieved, it is possible to receive the inner knowledge of Da'at.

By ascending the trunk of the Tree of Life, using the branches to help us in the process, we are assisted in returning to our Divine Source. This is the essence of following the Kabbalist pathway.

Concluding Comments

We have discussed the renewal of Kabbalistic teachings as well as the workings of the metaphysical Tree of Life and how it may be used to help us to re-runite with the Divine in our lives. Some of the key points deriving from this spiritual tradition include the following:

> *The universe is made out of the Source from which it was created. In Kabbalah this Source is called Ein Sof (Nothingness.)*

The Tree of Life gives a pictorial description of the qualities of Ein Sof which are also manifested through human beings.

Both restraint and expansion are necessary attributes of the Divine as well as of human beings. These are sometimes referred to as feminine and masculine qualities.

One begins to symbolically climb the Tree of Life when one becomes aware that there is potential within the physical world for uniting with that which is Divine.

As one begins to integrate the qualities associated with the Tree of Life, one becomes more and more in tune with the Divine.

By focusing on the sacred nature of all of life, one symbolically raises sparks of divinity, making the world a brighter place.

As human beings unite with God, or Ein Sof, co-creation of a better world becomes a natural process.

Personal Reflections

I first learned about the Kabbalah from Dr. Sheldon Kramer, who invited me to participate in a workshop by Rabbi Zalman Schacter (now known as Zalman Schacter-Shalomi). I attended the workshop and was quite impressed with the rabbi's way of introducing Kabbalistic teachings to both the Jews and non-Jews who were in attendance. I was especially excited about the way I felt during the chanting. It was as though I had discovered a place which was at the root of both Judaism and Christianity. I was invited to continue studying Kabbalah with Dr. Kramer, who had started a small study group, but felt, at the time, that I did not have enough knowledge of Judaism to really understand Kabbalah.

I later became exposed to Kabbalah again when I met Maura Richman, who had been a student of Dr. Kramer and was now continuing to teach those early students of his. She invited me to attend a lecture one evening by Rabbi David Cooper. I went to the lecture and found myself chanting again. Even though the Hebrew words in the chant were strange-sounding to me, I loved participating. It was wonderful and again gave me that feeling of being connected to something very ancient and beautiful. There is something special about chanting which cuts through the abstract and takes one directly to the core of whatever is being honored through that process. I decided to take a Kabbalah class with Maura, beginning in the fall of 1999 and continuing until the summer of 2000. In addition, I found myself reading as much as I could find about the subject. It was then that I decided to include the Path of Kabbalah in this book.

An aspect of Kabbalah, which has been exciting to me, is the beautiful imagery within its teachings. Much of this imagery reminds me of some of the poetry I have written in the past. I have come to appreciate that we are often given inspirational messages and images of possibilities which may be manifested later as physical realities in our lives. This happens when we are open and receptive to the creative process, allowing it the freedom to unfold in a natural, unhurried manner.

An example of tapping into universal themes through the intuitive creative process, I believe, may be found in a group of stories written by my friend and yoga teacher, Barbara Morse (also known as Ayosea). As mentioned earlier, Isaac Luria introduced the idea of vessels, which were created to contain the Sefirot. In the process, these vessels broke, scattering Ein Sof's sparks of light throughout the universe. Luria also spoke about the trapping of these sparks in shells or husks. When I first heard Luria's ideas, I was reminded of Morse's *Squnch* stories, which are part of an expressive arts program she developed. Two of the stories, *The Maestro Music Star* and *The Awakening of the Music Stars*, seem to be very similar to the Kabbalist Story of Creation.

Morse wrote that Music Stars, under the direction of a Maestro Music Star, had once filled the heavens with beautiful melodies. When a Careless Comet scattered them far and wide, many of the fragments of these stars landed in shells at the bottom of the sea. The Squnches were little beings who developed in these shells. When a storm pushed them into a beautiful valley, they came out of their shells and began the process of learning who they were. Eventually, they discovered the Music Stars within them, which gave them their true voices and helped them to realize their connection to something greater than themselves (the Maestro Music Star).

I believe that there is a mystical connection between Barbara's Music Stars and the Sefirot. In her story the stars were scattered far and wide, just like the Sefirot, and became attached to shells in the material universe. Just as the Squnches were awakened by the Music Stars within them, the Kabbalists tell us that we human beings may also be awakened by discovering the sparks of divinity within us. Morse's stories suggest that it is possible, through our creative imagination, to be divinely inspired and tap into a universal source of wisdom. This appears to be the same divine source from which the understanding and knowledge of Kabbalah emerged. This, to me, is very exciting and points to the importance of the creative process.

Another insight I received while studying the Kabbalah, is that the Shekhinah represents the Feminine Aspect of God. Two authors, who discuss the Shekhinah, are Andrew Harvey and Anne Baring. In their book, *The Divine feminine: Exploring the Feminine Face of God Around the World*, it is suggested that the Kabbalah has been responsible for bringing awareness of this feminine quality of God into Judaic/Christian traditions. It is indeed through the doorway of the Shekhinah that our physical world is connected to the realms of the Divine.

An author who points out connections between Judaism and Christianity is Elizabeth Clare Prophet. In her book, *Kabbalah: Keys to Inner Power,* she talks about Tiferet as being personified by Jesus Christ and the Shekhinah as representing the bride of Tiferet. In their symbolic marriage, the physical and divine realms are joined together. In our own lives, according to Prophet, we may help to bring the two together by honoring the Shekhinah within ourselves and allowing her to unite with Tiferet.

Practice Exercises

Tree of Life Exercise

We may use the Tree of Life in order to work with the energies within our own bodies and emotions. While looking at the illustration of the Tree of Life at the beginning of this chapter, imagine yourself standing and facing forward. In this way, the left side of the illustration corresponds to the left side of your body and the right side corresponds to the right side of your body. Likewise, the circles in the middle correspond to the center of your body.

The right column of the Tree of Life (corresponding to the masculine side of yourself) represents the expansive part of your nature. The left column (corresponding to the feminine side of yourself) represents the restraining part of your nature. The middle column contains Sefirot which harmonize the polarities from left and right, bringing out the best in both and also helping to balance their energies. In addition, these Sefirot represent the center of our bodies and lives, which align us with our creator.

The following meditation, based on the Tree of Life, may be used to deepen your understanding of the Path of Kabbalah by grounding the ideas within your body. It is presented from the ground up, so to speak, beginning by concentrating on Malkhut/Shekhinah, which is the Sefirot closest and most available to us, then ascending the Tree of Life. You may want to record the following instructions on an audio cassette and play them for yourself as you sit quietly and meditate. It is a good idea to keep a pen and paper handy so you can write down your experiences afterward.

Close your eyes and concentrate on your feet, as they ground you in Mother Earth or Malkhut. Express your gratitude to the Great Mother, which has given you your life. Let her know that you will tread lightly upon her and always respect her. Now allow an image of the Divine Feminine, or Shekhinah, to come to you, bathed in holy light. Bask in the light of her loving protection, which has been with you since the beginning of time and will always be present with you. Trust in her sacred protection as you approach the doorway to the Tree of Life.

Now concentrate on the pelvic area of your body (representing your sense of self, which has been developed in Yesod). It is here that you have learned to harmonize the hard-working aspect of Netzach with the receptive aspect of Hod in order to create a stable foundation. What kind of foundation are you building? Is it one which will be firm and strong in the midst of turmoil? Can you act meaningfully in the world? Allow yourself to feel a strong foundation which you are creating with the help of the divine assistance found in the Tree of Life.

Now concentrate on your left hip and leg, the place of Hod. Hod gives you the ability to receive the good things in life to which you are entitled. As you rest here in Hod, allow yourself to release any stresses or strains you may feel in your body, or concerns which you may have in your mind. Just let them all go as you sit and allow yourself to be still, without doing anything. You may be surprised at what the universe has in store for you when you are quiet enough to receive her gifts. Hod also gives you the intuition which allows you to monitor your willful pursuit of goals in a balanced manner.

Now concentrate on your right hip and leg, the place of Netzach, which gives you the perisitence and endurance you need to reach your goals. Form a picture in your mind of your goals and what you need to do in order to achieve them. Here, in Netzach, you are given the endurance that you need to accomplish those things which will make your goals a reality.

Now concentrate your awareness in your heart, the place of Tiferet. Allow the beauty of Tiferet to shine through in whatever way that is appropriate for you. Feel the harmony located here, as well as a great compassion for all that is. Feel at home here in your heart with Tiferet as you allow the loving-kindness of Chesed and the discipline of Gevurah to come into harmony and balance. Spend some time with your True Self here in Tiferet. Experience a feeling of well-being and peace. It is here that all of the Sefirot are harmonized and synthesized in your life.

Now place your awareness on your left shoulder and arm. Feel the restraint and discipline of Gevurah here, as it gives you a feeling of strength and power. Note any areas of your life in which you need to set limits or boundaries. Give yourself permission to say "no" when it is in your best interest and the best interest of others to do so.

Now concentrate on your right shoulder and arm, which represents the loving-kindness of Chesed. Enjoy the warm glow of Chesed as you bask in its light and feel nurtured and greatly loved. Are there people in your life who need to feel more of your love? Do you need to feel more love from them? Do you need to love yourself more than you do? Concentrate on the quality of loving-kindness and discover those areas of your life where it is present and those areas where it may be needed. Also note those areas in which it may have been excessive and in need of containment.

Now bring your awareness to the area between your eyebrows, sometimes referred to as the third eye. Find that unique place which is like a sacred chamber into which you may enter and gain the great knowledge of Da'at. Wisdom and understanding have given way to knowledge here. Allow yourself to be open to the source of true knowledge. What is revealed to you as you visit Da'at, the place of inner knowing?

Now concentrate on the left side of your brain. It is here, with Binah, the Divine Mother, that new insights and understandings become clear to you. You may receive an image of a light, a particular color, or a wise person. If you want to, you may choose to ask Binah a question concerning your life and your true purpose on earth.

Now concentrate on the right side of your brain. Allow your mind to relax and enjoy the intuitive and inspirational wisdom of Chochmah, the Divine Father. Sense the wisdom which exists in the inner realms of your mind as you simply relax and be with that which is indefinable and divine within yourself. Note any images, sounds, or colors which come to you as you sit in the seat of your wisdom and simply receive whatever gifts are there for you.

Now imagine a light above the top of your head. As you unify with the light of Keter, feel a connection to your Divine Source. It is here that you are always united with All That Is. Your divinity has been kept unspoiled for you and is waiting for your return. Now allow that light to pour through your head, streaming throughout your body, unifying you with everything in the universe and giving you a feeling of bliss and great peace. When you are ready, open your eyes and return to the place where you began this exercise.

Pamela Allen

Chapter Six
Jesus and the Christ Within

While traveling down this pathway, we are invited to follow the teachings of Jesus, who was so identified with his spiritual nature that he became known as The Christ. The Christ Within refers to that part of ourselves which is true and divine in nature. It was in this holy place within himself that Jesus and The Father (God) were one. It is in this holy place within ourselves that we, too, may experience oneness with our creator. The dove of peace represents the Holy Spirit, symbolic of God's love for all beings.

109

Jesus And The Christ Within

Overview

Each chapter in this book discusses a spiritual pathway which promotes a feeling of peace within the minds and hearts of those who practice it. This particular chapter deals with the life and teachings of Jesus Christ, whose message continues to touch millions of people around the globe. I have entitled it *Jesus and the Christ Within* in order to highlight, not only the historical Jesus, who walked and talked on the earth approximately 2000 years ago, but also the Jesus who speaks to the hearts of many of his followers even today with a *still, small voice*. When Jesus left this earthly plane, he told his disciples that he would send a Comforter to them, to guide them always. I like to think of the Comforter as The Christ Within, who continues to communicate with those of his followers who are quiet and receptive enough to receive his messages.

Regardless of how he is viewed, Jesus left a profound legacy in the world as we know it. Indeed, the calendar most of us have been using in the western world for many years is based on the estimated date of his birth on our planet. Some of his followers are Orthodox Christians, who accept the New Testament of the Bible as the authoritative text of their religion. Adherents of this viewpoint believe that Jesus was the Christ, or Messiah, who came to earth as a direct manifestation of God.

In contrast to the Orthodox Christian viewpoint, there is another, more modern viewpoint, which suggests that Jesus was a Master Teacher, who taught those who would listen to him, that all human beings are sons and daughters of God. Since Jesus had fully realized his own sense of divinity, he was entitled, according to this viewpoint, to be called Christ.

We begin our discussion by viewing Jesus in the light of history. His life and teachings, as well as the legacy he left with those who carry on his teachings, are discussed. In this context, we take a look at the Christian movement as it has grown out of Judaism and changed over the years to become a distinct religion of its own.

Next, we take a look at two important discoveries. One is a set of scrolls found near the Dead Sea during the late 1940's and early 50's known as the Dead Sea Scrolls. The other is a set of papyrus documents discovered in 1945 in a place in upper Egypt known as Nag Hammadhi. There has been a great deal of controversy surrounding these discoveries. Also included in this chapter is a description of some of the personal encounters with Jesus, or the Christ Within, which have been reported throughout history.

As stated in the Introduction, it is a tenet of this book that many spiritual pathways intersect and contain universal threads of similarity. You may note as you read this chapter that there are some similarities, for example, between the teachings of Jesus and the teachings of Buddha. This gives support to the notion that there may indeed be universal threads which hold them together.

Historical Perspectives on Christianity

According to the King James Version of the Bible, Jesus was born in Bethlehem and grew up in Nazareth, near the Sea of Galilee. He was born to Jewish parents at a time when Jews were subjects of the Roman Empire. As long as they showed proper respect for Roman law, they were allowed to practice their religion. The only Jewish temple at that time was in Jerusalem, a city considered to be the center of Judaic faith. Jews from all around the area would make pilgrimages to Jerusalem to celebrate their holy days.

Although he was born into a modest family, Jesus became an influential teacher, traveling from place to place, teaching the people to love God and to love each other. He also taught them that the kingdom of God was within them. Jesus was known as a great healer and people would come from miles around to receive his healing power, which he said came from God. Jesus taught the people with parables and metaphors. He later explained the parables in more detail to his twelve disciples, who are said to have traveled with him during those times.

Jesus taught his followers that the most important thing in the world is love. He told them to love God with all their hearts and to love others, even those considered to be their enemies, as much as they loved themselves. He told them to do good to everyone and to forgive those who had hurt them. He taught them to judge not or they themselves would be judged. Jesus said that there is a spiritual kingdom, which is everlasting, in addition to the earthly kingdom, which is transient. His teachings were about trusting God to look after their needs and about becoming unattached to the things of the world.

The four books of the Bible which are known as the Gospels are Matthew, Mark, Luke, and John. These books tell us that Jesus went with his disciples to Jerusalem for the Jewish Passover. Apparently it was during this time that he was arrested by the Romans and eventually put to death by crucifixion. Biblical scholars have suggested that the Romans saw Jesus as dangerous because he spoke about bringing the kingdom of God to earth. Since the Romans viewed their empire as the only legitimate and ultimate kingdom on earth, this was threatening to their belief system and to the authority of Rome.

It is said in the Bible that Jesus arose from the dead three days after his crucifixion and subsequent burial. It is also said that, after his death, he appeared in the flesh to his disciples, instructing them to go out and preach his Gospel of love and forgiveness. Jesus's followers did teach his message to those Jews who would listen to them. Later they also shared it with the Gentiles (non-Jews). They taught people that Jesus had died for their sins and that, by believing in him as their Savior, they, too, could have eternal life.

The history of the Christian movement is very interesting. It was depicted recently on a television series entitled *2000 Years of Christianity* sponsored by American Century. One of the highlighted points was that the followers of Jesus developed a new sect within Judaism. They were probably known as the "Jesus people." Unlike the Pharisees, who had come into power within Judaism, these people believed that Jesus of Nazareth was the Messiah who had come to save them from their sins. The more traditional Jews did not accept this notion and tended to look upon the "Jesus people" as being misguided. A rift began to grow between the new sect of Judaism and the more traditional branch. For instance, there was disagreement regarding the law of circumcision. Gentile males, who had joined the movement, did not feel that they needed to be circumcised but the traditional Jews felt that they should be. Another Jewish law was that no work should be done on the Sabbath. Jesus taught his disciples, however, that it was acceptable to heal those who were sick even if it was the Sabbath. The differences between the two groups became irreconcilable and, by the beginning of the first century, they had broken apart. This was considered to be the beginning of Christianity as a religious movement, distinct from Judaism.

According to the BRAVO series, many Christians were persecuted during the second and third centuries because they would not make sacrifices to the Roman gods. Some them became willing martyrs for the cause of their movement. Instead of hurting the movement, this martyrdom actually strengthened it. By the latter part of the third century, Christianity had grown and spread into many regions. For example, in Egypt, the majority of the people had already become Christian. In the fourth century, the Roman leader, Constantine, after dreaming about their power to help him in battle, became sympathetic to the Christians. He became a Christian himself and donated money for churches to be built in Constantinople. Over time, there tended to be a blending of Roman and Christian traditions. For instance, the Sabbath was moved to Sunday, instead of Saturday. Other Christian holidays were moved to dates which coincided with pagan festivals (Easter and Christmas for example). Christians, who had started out as part of Judaism, began to appear more like the Romans than like the Jews.

As Christianity developed over the years, many followers began to focus more on Jesus as a deity rather than Jesus as a teacher. Within Christianity, the Roman Catholic Church eventually developed and the Pope, or leader of the Church, was considered to have spiritual authority over all Christians. In 1517, Martin Luther launched the Protestant Reformation, which occurred as a rebellion against the authority of the Pope. The Protestant churches which developed, also became divided into different denominations. Today, some fundamental Protestant churches are very literal in their interpretation of the Bible. Other denominations see the Bible stories as more symbolic in nature.

Recent Discoveries and New Viewpoints

In looking at the development of Christianity, let us take into account two important discoveries which occurred near the middle of the twentieth century. The first is the discovery of the Dead Sea Scrolls in a cave near the Dead Sea. The second is the discovery of what is now known as the Nag Hammadhi Library.

Some, but not all, of the material from the Dead Sea Scrolls has been published and is thought by scholars to have been written by a Jewish sect known as the Essenes. According to Larson (*The Essene-Christian Faith: A Study in the Sources of Western Religion),* the Essenes, prior to the birth of Jesus, had gone out from Jerusalem to live a very monastic life in the remote countryside. Believing that the priests in the temple at Jerusalem had become politically corrupt, they sought a way of practicing their faith in what they felt to be a purer form. They were communal and celibate in their lifestyle.

Larson and other scholars of today believe that Jesus may have been a member of the Essene Order of Jews before he started his teaching ministry. The reason for this assumption is that he fulfilled a prophesy which they held close to their hearts, that a Messiah would come to earth, become the spiritual leader of the Jews, and would then be killed to atone for their sins. After three days, he would arise from the dead and go to live with God, preparing the way for those who believed in him to have eternal life. Since the Bible describes Jesus as having done all of these things, there may be some truth to the theory that he was, indeed, an Essene.

The Nag Hammadhi Library consists of fifty-two papyrus documents, which were discovered in Egypt. According to Elaine Pagels, who wrote *The Gnostic Gospels,* an Arab peasant known as Muhammad Ali discovered them by the Nile River. He tried to make money on them by selling them as antiquities and the documents did not come to the public eye until about thirty years later. Scholars now believe that they were written by the ancient Gnostics, a sect within the early Christian movement.

Who were the Gnostics? According to *Encarta: World English Dictionary,* the word, "gnostic" means "relating to knowledge, especially knowledge of spiritual truths." It comes from the Greek word "gnosis," which means "investigation, knowledge." "Gnosticism" is defined in the same dictionary as "a pre-Christian and early Christian religious movement teaching that salvation comes by learning esoteric spiritual truths that free humanity from the material world, believed in this movement to be evil."

Most Orthodox Christians viewed the Gnostics as heretics because they did not deify Jesus as the only son of God. Instead, they viewed him more as a guide and teacher who came to show humanity how to find God within themselves. Because this teaching was so similar to the teachings of Buddhism and Hinduism, some modern scholars speculate that Jesus had traveled to India during the period in his life which is not reported in the Bible. Some of the myths associated with Gnosticism are also similar to those from ancient Egypt, Greece and Rome.

The goal of life, according to the Gnostics, is to tune into the truths of the universe which may be found within. "Gnosis" is based on intuitive insights rather than rational thinking. When one knows in one's heart that something is true, it is not necessary to prove it scientifically, according to this system. The truth of God, according to the Gnostics, is described as being within the human soul or spirit, rather than through any organized religion. This truth, they say, may be realized through meditation and receptivity to a higher power which speaks directly to the soul. Some might say today that the *Course in Miracles* is based on such a belief system. (There will be more discussion on the *Course in Miracles* later in this chapter.)

Stephan Hoeller wrote a book which compared Gnosticism with some of the theories of Carl Jung. It is entitled *Jung and the Lost Gospels*. He indicates that the material discovered in the Dead Sea Scrolls about the Jewish Essenes, as well as the Gnostic material found within the Nag Hammadhi Library, are spiritually similar and are congruent with Jung's teachings. Jung's depth psychology deals with bringing light to the darkness in the soul. Hoeller feels that the Gnostics' emphasis on bringing God's light to earth is similar in nature to Jung's theoretical system, though on a spiritual, rather than psychological level.

There are some followers of Jesus's teachings today, who are considered to be outside the traditional forms of Christianity because they do not see Christianity as an exclusive pathway to God. This would be the case, for example, in some of the New Thought churches today, such as the Church of Religious Science and the Unity Church. People who follow the New Thought religions tend to believe that Jesus came as a teacher, messenger, and example for others to follow. They would generally agree that he demonstrated by his life and teachings what it means to be an expression of perfect love on earth. Unlike Orthodox Christians, however, they would not tend to consider that belief in Jesus is the only way to reach God. Following the teachings of Buddha, for example, would be considered another way.

Throughout history, destructive forces have been unleashed in the world in the name of religious beliefs. Rather than using religions to promote separation, fear, and wars on our planet, might it be possible to use the universal teachings from these religions to promote unity, love, and peace? Along these lines, Ken Carey tells us in his book, *Terra Christa: The Global Spiritual Awakening*, that Jesus's teachings are similar to the teachings of the Buddha. For example, Jesus taught his followers to recognize their faults, have a genuine desire to change, and to pursue their livelihoods in a gentle, humble, nonviolent way, showing compassion for all people. This is very much like what the Buddha taught his followers. Unconditional love for all beings is the ultimate teaching in both Buddhism and Christianity. If human beings can ever learn to express this kind of love on a global scale, there will be no need for wars or hunger on our planet.

Two authors, one a Christian, the other a Buddhist, wrote books in which the teachings of Christ and Buddha were compared. The Christian author, Marcus Borg, in his book, *Jesus and Buddha: The Parallel Sayings*, brings out the point that both Buddha and Christ started renewal movements in their religions (Judaism and Hinduism), creating Christianity and Buddhism as a result. He also suggested that neither saw himself as a founder of a religion but rather as a teacher of truth.

The Buddhist author, Thich Nhat Hanh, writes in his book, *Living Buddha, Living Christ,* about the need in our world for cultures to dialogue with one another so that all may learn to live in peace and evolve in a positive way. He compares the mindfulness associated with Buddhism with the Holy Spirit associated with Christianity. Mindfulness helps one to love more deeply and bring about healing in one's life. Likewise, the Holy Spirit is considered to be that aspect of God which guides one to a higher purpose in life.

Christ Encounters

Personal encounters with Christ have been reported throughout the ages and even in recent times. One of the people who reported mystical encounters with Christ is the Roman Catholic nun and mystic, Anne Catherine Emerick, who bore the stigmata of Jesus's crucifixion on her body. In other words, wounds developed on her hands, feet, and head like those Jesus bore during his crucifixion. She would go into trances and receive visions of various events in Jesus's life, as though she were actually present.

As recorded in Volume One of the book, *The Life of Jesus Christ and Biblical Revelations,* Sister Anne describes a vision of Jesus which she had while deep in prayer. He came offering her either a crown of thorns or a crown of flowers. She chose the crown of thorns because she wanted to share the pain which Jesus had suffered. Her visions were accompanied by physical pain, which she willingly accepted and considered to be part of her devotion to Jesus. She was unable to leave her bed during the latter part of her life and reportedly, for much of the time, could only eat or drink the Holy Eucharist (bread and wine of communion in the Catholic Church, believed to be transformed into the flesh and blood of Jesus Christ upon consecration). During these times, she would meditate, go into ecstatic states of mind, and have vivid visions of various events from Jesus's life. She could hear the voices of Jesus and the others around him. She also felt the pains of some of the people who came to her for spiritual help. Sensitive to their sufferings, she would often take on their physical symptoms and suffer with them. Despite her physical sufferings, she appeared to others to be at peace with herself and with the path she had chosen. As a result, she was an inspiration to many people.

In reading through the accounts of Sister Anne's meditations, I was amazed at the vividness of her descriptions of external and internal events taking place. It was as if she were actually living at the time of Jesus and giving a verbal account of the events as they occurred around her. Her accounts included, for example, the experience of being beside Jesus's manger when he was a baby. She could actually feel, within her own body, a fever which he was having. She also experienced what it was like later on for him and his family when they were hungry. Referring to Jesus as her Beloved Spouse, she was also present, in a vision, at the time of his crucifixion and subsequent resurrection.

Another person who claimed to receive messages from Christ was the French woman, Gabrielle Bossis. In her book, *He and I,* Bossis claimed to have had many inner conversations with Christ during the course of her daily activities. Evelyn M. Brown, who translated the book into English, tells us that Bossis heard what she referred to as "The Voice" when she was young, but did not begin to take it seriously until she was in her sixties. "The Voice" which she heard encouraged her to help others and to see Christ in their faces. It also encouraged her to publish her material so that people would know that intimacy with Christ was possible for the ordinary person, and not only for monks and nuns living in monasteries. First published in 1948 anonymously, *He and I* became widely distributed. Because it was so popular, a second volume was printed prior to her death in 1950 in which Bossis's identity was revealed.

Many modern accounts of encounters with Jesus have also been reported. For example, an artist by the name of Glenda Green reports that Jesus appeared to her as she was painting a portrait of him in 1992. In the process of having his portrait painted, Jesus taught her many beautiful lessons, which she recorded on several audio cassettes and later included in her book, entitled *Love Without End: Jesus Speaks.*

Green states in her book that her husband had received a dream that she was to paint a portrait of Jesus. At the time, she was an artist but had not done any religious paintings. She indicated to him playfully that she would paint Jesus only if he showed up to be her model. To her surprise, one afternoon after waking up from a deep sleep, she noticed that the room was filled with light. A beam of light was shot from a particularly lighted area of the room to her forehead and, in her mind's eye, a vision of the painting she was to do was implanted. Green explains in her book that when she started to paint the picture, she was wondering how to hold the image in her mind while actually painting the picture. At that point, Jesus appeared to be standing there in front of her. He manifested before her each time she entered her studio to work on the portrait. Green reports that he eventually spoke to her as well. She painted the portrait over a period of about four months. During this time, she was able to ask Jesus questions and to receive responses. The most important teaching that he gave her was that human beings are rays of love which comes from God, who may be defined as Love Itself. Jesus also taught her that the heart, rather than the mind, is the place of true intelligence and that the Sacred Heart is the point within human beings where the physical, emotional, intellectual, and spiritual aspects of ourselves are in perfect alignment. It is in this place where communion with God is possible.

Another encounter with Jesus is described by Paul Ferrini who claims to have joined with the Christ Mind within his own mind in order to write a practical and beautiful guidebook for living a loving, spiritual life. The book is entitled *Love Without Conditions: Reflections of the Christ Mind*. Ferrini suggests that Jesus speaks to people through their minds, sometimes in words, and sometimes through images. He describes the Christ Mind as the place where other master teachers, such as Krishna and Buddha, join with Jesus. Those who are receptive to the teachings also join with these spiritual guides in the Christ Mind. Within each person, according to Ferrini, there is a spark of light which reveals the contents of his or her unconscious mind. This divine spark of awareness, he suggests, connects each person to God.

The author, Scott Sparrow, collected numerous accounts from people who claimed to have had personal encounters with Jesus, either through dreams or through visions. He divided them into different categories: spiritual awakening, physical or emotional healing, and confrontations or instructions. I was very moved by reading Sparrow's book, *I Am With You Always: True Stories of Encounters with Jesus,* listed in the reference section.

Perhaps the best known modern work, which originated from a personal encounter with Jesus, is the *Course in Miracles*. It is not only a textbook for life, but also includes daily lessons and a teacher's manual. The *Course in Miracles* is said to have been spiritually dictated by Jesus to a professor of psychology by the name of Helen Schucman, in order to give to the world a new framework for understanding and practicing his teachings.

In the *Course in Miracles,* Jesus speaks of the Holy Spirit, as being present within us, available always to guide us toward lives of peace, harmony, and love. The Holy Spirit is often depicted as a dove, which also represents the quality of peace.

The *Course in Miracles* has become a meaningful and practical spiritual pathway for many people in the United States and other countries around the world. By living lives filled with love and forgiveness, its followers strive to give up fear and know peace within themselves. Marianne Williamson's book, *A Return to Love*, gives a description of the *Course in Miracles* and some of its important concepts.

Since Jesus had totally actualized the Christ Mind within himself, he was in a position to help others do so. The *Course in Miracles* is said to have been dictated by Jesus for this purpose. It teaches that love is a natural tendency, whereas fear is something that we, as human beings, have learned because of our feeling of separation from God. This spiritual pathway involves releasing fear and inviting love back into our lives. When we do this, we align with God's will in order to co-create our lives. Christ, according to the *Course in Miracles*, represents the divine love which is within all beings. Accepting the Christ Within is also accepting ourselves as divine creatures.

Concluding Comments

Some of the key points from this spiritual pathway include the following:

Jesus taught that God loves human beings unconditionally.

God has been described as Love Itself, while human beings are described as individualized manifestations of that Love.

People throughout the ages claim to have received guidance from Jesus.

It is possible to unite with Jesus and other spiritual masters by tuning into the Christ Within.

Christ Consciousness leads one to love others without judgment or conditions.

Heaven is the state of mind in which one is united with God.

The Kingdom of God may be found within oneself.

Personal Reflections

Of all the chapters in this book, this one is the closest to my heart. As a little child, I was taught that Jesus was my spiritual friend who would always be there to comfort me in times of need. This became so important to me as I grew older that I wanted to become a missionary and teach people around the world about him. I even considered at one point what it might be like to become a nun, but I wasn't Catholic and that didn't make any sense.

When I went to college, I followed my spiritual interest by studying religions from around the world. This opened my eyes to the fact that there are many pathways leading to God. I could no longer accept the limited view that there is only one pathway, for it leaves out too many people from too many cultures. I eventually settled on the field of psychology as a career path, but continued to explore theories in psychology which embraced the spiritual, as well as psychological paths in life.

Though I was moving away from participation in organized religion, I remember going through the Bible and writing down passages which still had meaning for me. I put Jesus's teachings away in a corner of my heart, where they would not resurface until many years later. When I discovered Zen Buddhism and the power of meditation, a spiritual void, which I felt in my life after abandoning Christianity, was once again filled. I later studied Tai Chi and explored Native American spiritual teachings. All of these pathways enriched my soul and gave me a greater awareness of my connection to the spiritual side of life. I still wondered how Jesus fit into the big picture, however, and I missed the connection with him that I had felt as a child.

Being interested in spiritual, as well as psychological growth, I naturally gravitated toward the theories of Carl Gustav Jung, who seemed to be able to blend the two. Jung was considered by many to be a mystic. He was interested not only in the positive aspects of God, but also in the dark aspects of the psyche's journey toward wholeness. His father was a minister and his mother a psychic. He sought, I think, to bring what he had learned from both parents together. I, too, have had a desire to bridge psychology with spirituality because they have both been pathways leading me to a feeling of wholeness and authenticity in life.

Happening upon the book, *The Gnostic Jung and the Seven Sermons to the Dead,* by Stephan Hoeller, I was fascinated with Hoeller's suggestion that

Carl Jung was connected to the early Gnostics. He made reference to a book, written by Jung, entitled *Seven Sermons to the Dead*. This book had not been published for the general public until the first English translation of it was completed in 1925. It is interesting that Jung gave credit for the writing of the book to an early Gnostic leader by the name of Basilides. Some say that Jung, for fear that the psychological community would shun him for his interest in spiritual matters, did not want to announce to the public that he had written such a book. Others say that it is possible that the spirit of Basilides, in some way, "channeled" the book through Jung. Many scholars suggest that Jung, like the early Gnostics, was in touch with the quest for something lost. The Gnostics called this the "Pleroma" (a place which embraces the fullness of authentic being). "Gnosis" is an inner knowing that such a state exists and may actually be found by receiving guidance from within.

In addition to my psychological exploration, I also began to read the *Course in Miracles* in 1992 and found that something in my heart resonated with its teachings. I liked the idea that Jesus could have spoken to someone in modern times to offer guidance for those of us living today. I studied the *Course in Miracles* on my own and attended group gatherings where the teachings were discussed. It seemed to be a bridge for me, leading back to Jesus, but framed in a more universal package which my heart could accept. Jesus taught, through the *Course in Miracles*, that the Holy Spirit is available as a guide to us if we will only seek its guidance in our lives.

During 1992 and then again in 1995, I actively studied the *Course in Miracles* and would often take time to meditate after reading the lessons of the day. Eventually, while in a quiet, receptive state of mind, I began asking for messages from the Holy Spirit, which would help me along my spiritual pathway. Whereas I tend to "hear" messages when I ask for guidance, others report that they receive "pictures." Others report having feelings of bliss, of being comforted, and of feeling at one with the universe. There are many ways for inner guidance to be received. The important thing is to believe that it is possible to receive guidance and to take the time to ask for it.

The following messages are examples of the kind of guidance which I received when I opened myself up to the teachings of the *Course in Miracles*.

The following message had to do with my awakening to the inner guidance available to me:

"I am waking up inside of you, opening my eyes wide with wonder, seeing the beauty in life as it manifests and unfolds. I am the Spirit of Love that stands in awe over the cradle of a newborn baby, whose radiance fills the room and melts even the hardest of hearts. I am the breath of the wind, cooling the dusty faces of the toilers. I am the dew of early morning, bathing the earth in her own wonder. I breathe through the poor as well as the wealthy. I am the rose and it's fragrance, the songbird and his song. Sing with me the joyful Song of Creation. Together we awaken in every soul, enlivening that which was not dead, but only sleeping. Dance with me across the deserts. Fly with me to the ends of the earth and up, up, up to the very stars which await our coming. My spirit rises in you and will not be blocked this time around. I fill your heart with radiant, overflowing love. Words cannot describe the joy of my Presence. The smile spreading across your lips expresses the peace and love that I bring. Your tear drops are happy stars of light, melting in the warmth of my beingness within you. And so it is and always shall be."

The next message gave me instruction in how to distinguish true spiritual guidance from other voices inside my head.

"Be still and know that I am here to guide you. Listen for the one voice within which does not waver and which is clear and true. Calm your mind so that all the clatter can dissolve and you can hear the Voice of Wisdom within you."

The following message referred to the power of love:

"Love is natural energy radiating out from God, filling to overflowing, those who are open and receptive. This loving energy radiates through one's being and overflows into the world, touching and healing those with whom it comes into contact, filling them also with light, radiance, and love until the whole universe is lighted once again and all beings realize their divine nature. People move toward this light and joyful radiance, to feel its warmth. No one wants to be in darkness. It is not a natural state. Lighted love is healing. It fills and makes whole. It is unconditional because it needs nothing in return. It is sufficient unto itself. It is as natural as breathing. Unconditional love is pure joy given freely by God. It is inexhaustible and available to all who are open to allow it to flow freely through their lives."

The next message had to do with the nature of my function on earth:

"It's not about doing. It's about being....being totally in the moment with whatever you are doing... being fully present. That is what brings peace and joy to your soul. The other goals you set for yourself do not matter so much as your being fully present in those activities as they unfold. Listen within for the messages you receive as you go about your life and you will know when you are in the moment and when you are not."

The following message had to do with heaven on earth:

"Heaven is opening up to you. Embrace it as your own experience, for heaven is truly a state of your mind, free from clutter and focused on the one true nature of your beingness. Heaven is bliss. It is with you at all times as you simply turn your attention to the truth of who you are. Enjoy your inheritance. Take time to turn inward and embrace the good which is yours to receive and share with others. Go now in peace and the peace of God goes with you."

The following message had to do with freedom:

"I am the Voice from deep within, reminding you that you are much more than you know. You are expanded to include the entire universe and more. You are flowing through life with this expanded state of awareness now, knowing that you are vast and inclusive, not limited by your little body. You are living on the inner planes of reality as well as in the physical realm. Relax and

> *flow in this awareness and enjoy the feeling of being unlimited and unhindered, completely free and whole, filled with joy, light, beauty, love, and compassion."*

I feel that the above messages are from my own connection with the Christ Mind, which may also be described as the "gnosis," or inner wisdom, within me. I have derived a great deal of comfort in knowing that this guidance is available to me whenever I am open enough to receive it. I feel loved and cared for in the inner, spiritual realms of my existence, as well as in the outer, physical realm. In fact, it seems that the two dimensions have actually worked together to bring about more love, peace, healing, and freedom in my life. For example, I have learned that, when uncomfortable or distressed, I can turn things around in a positive direction by consciously tuning into the connection I feel with the Christ Within.

I once again recognized wisdom inside myself in March, 1999, while being with my mother when she died. After a tortuous night of struggling between life and death, she seemed quiet and peaceful in the early hours of that last day of her life, which happened to be on Palm Sunday. Both my sister and I sensed her spirit as it left her weary body and took flight with what appeared to be a Holy Presence. Later, as I left the hospital, a large bird swooped before me and flew upward into the sky. I smiled, recognizing this as a symbol of my mother's spirit, which had been set free.

Practice Exercises

Course in Miracles

Try reading the *Course in Miracles* workbook. There is an exercise included in each daily lesson to ground the lesson more fully. When you practice the lessons, be open to receiving guidance from an inner place of wisdom.

Meditation

Use some form of meditation to quiet your mind of all its chatter. Allow your mind to join with the Christ Mind. Receive the guidance available to you.

Music

Listen to some beautiful meditative music. Close your eyes and let your mind relax. If visions appear, enjoy receiving them. Perhaps you will want to paint a picture of your visions or write a beautiful poem, expressing their meaning to you. Let your creation be an expression of the "gnosis" (knowledge) within you.

Nature

Take a walk in a beautiful setting where you feel at peace. Notice everything (trees, rocks, flowers, shells, and sky). Feel the wind across your face. Enjoy the fragrance of nature. See each part of nature as an expression of the Christ Mind, reflecting back to you your own special qualities. Send out your love to everything you see. Feel it returned to you. This is the circle of life.

Visualization

Walk down a street and look at each person you meet, seeing the light of Christ within each one. See how this awakens your spirit and brings joy to your soul.

Beauty

Go out to view the sunrise and/or sunset. Feel the radiance of the sun as it permeates your being. Imagine it is the light within your own being, radiating outward into the world around you.

Chapter Seven
Sufism

Along the Sufi path, attempts are made to purify our hearts so that the we may reunite with The Beloved (Allah). The spiral represents Allah's creation of the universe (clockwise from the center out), as well as our return to Allah. The Whirling Dervishes' dance symbolizes this process.

Sufism

Introduction

What is Sufism? This is a question which has been answered in many ways by different authors and teachers. The most common definition seems to be that it is the "mystical aspect of Islam." What is Islam? Briefly, it is a religion based on the teachings of the Prophet, Muhammad, to whom the Holy *Qur'an* (Koran) is said to have been divinely revealed, beginning in the early 7th century and continuing over the course of his life. Some say that the *Qur'an* came to Muhammad through the Archangel, Gabriel. Others say that it came directly from God, or Allah, as God is called in the Islamic faith.

Since Muhammad was not formally educated, he could not write down the revelations he had received. Instead, he taught them orally to his followers, who compiled the material later into the written form of the *Qur'an*. The followers of Islam became known as Muslims. Among them were some who were particularly devout and mystically-oriented. They longed to experience directly the kind of union with God which Muhammad had experienced. Because they wore coarse, woolen garments like other religious ascetics of the day, they eventually became called Sufis. (Suf, in Arabic, means wool). Prior to that they were referred to as pious followers of Muhammad, concerning themselves with the inner mystical essence of what he was saying (rather than the outer form of the Islamic faith which was to evolve out of his teachings).

The Sufis were impressed that Muhammad had experienced a mystical reunion with God and they, too, desired such an experience. In this respect, they were similar to the Gnostics of early Christianity who wanted to have the same relationship with God that Jesus had experienced. Sufis are also similar to the early Kabbalists, or mystics within Judaism, which we explored in Chapter Five. Sufis, Gnostics, and Kabbalists have all expressed this deep longing to have an intimate relationship with God while living in the physical world.

When Sufis open themselves up to God, they experience a Divine Light in the center of their being. Llewellyn Vaughan-Lee, in an audio tape, entitled *The Sufi Path of Love: How Longing Leads to the Ecstasy of Divine Union*, tells us that the expression "light upon light" is often used to express the experience of God's light filling the Sufi's heart. The Sufi's light then rises to meet God's greater light which shines out on the world. In the 24th sura (chapter) of the *Qur'an* this concept of "light upon light" is expressed beautifully. The emphasis on light is one which is found in Judaism and Christianity, in addition to the Islamic faith.

Though Sufis value intuitive knowledge and mystical experiences, the most important quality they strive to activate within their lives is love. Indeed, the essence of Sufism is a deep love for God, whom they refer to as The Beloved. It is said that a person who enters this path has an intuitive memory of having been with God before and experiences a deep longing to return home. The journey, once begun, is a gradual process of releasing attachments to the material world so that a spiritual reunion with the Divine may take place.

Vaughan-Lee tells us in his audio tape that Sufis often refer to God as "he" even though they do not think of God as having any gender at all. This is because the human soul, which longs for God, is viewed by the Sufis as being feminine in nature. Men and women are both viewed as having masculine and feminine qualities and so the "love affair" between the soul (represented by the feminine) and God (represented by the masculine) takes place in both men and women. Sufis also refer to God as Friend. This is because of the intimacy which they feel with their creator. They also see aspects of God in each other and, therefore, refer to other Sufis as friends along the path.

Those who follow the Sufi Path seek to purify their hearts and souls so that God, The Beloved, will see fit to live within them. They strive to release their egos so that nothing is left within their hearts but God's presence. This is similar to the concept in Hinduism of the birth of the Atman (God Within) which we discussed at length in Chapter Three.

Historical Framework

As mentioned earlier, Sufism has its roots in the Islamic faith, brought forth by the Prophet Muhammad. The *Qur'an* is said to have been divinely revealed to Muhammad, beginning while he was on a spiritual retreat in a cave near Mecca. Muhammad had gone there to seek guidance from God in order to help the Arabs to live a more spiritual lifestyle.

Thomas Lippman, in his book, *Understanding Islam: An Introduction to the Muslim World*, tells us that Muhammad was born during the sixth century in Mecca, a city in Saudi Arabia. The people there worshipped many gods as well as idols at that time. There was a shrine in Mecca which had been built to honor these gods and idols. It was known as the Kaaba. Later, after Muhammad introduced the concept of One God (Allah) to the Arabs, this shrine became Islamic and represented a common place where Muslims from all over the world could come and feel their brotherhood, as Muslims. Lippman also tells us that, in addition to the *Qur'an*, the *Hadith*, a collection of Muhammad's sayings, is also considered to be sacred in nature. Those who follow the Islamic teachings, based on the *Qur'an* and the *Hadith*, accept a belief in One God.

In addition to following other ethical teachings, there are five main requirements in Islam. These include: (1) to believe that there is one God

(Allah) and that Muhammad is God's Messenger, (2) to pray to Allah five times a day, (3) to fast during the daylight hours of the month of Ramadan, (4) to give a certain percentage of goods to the poor at the end of the month of Ramadan, and (5) to make a pilgrimage to Mecca at least once in their lives if able to do so. Huston Smith gives a good description of the development of Islam in his book,*The world's Religions: Our Great Wisdom Traditions.*

Development and Expansion

By the 10th Century, Sufism had expanded into Spain and Western Europe. Engaged in mystical practices, patterned after those of Muhammad, Sufis attempted to bring together the realms of spirit and matter. Like the Hindu ascetics, they often went door to door, begging for food and a place to stay. For this reason, thery were often referred to as wandering dervishes. According to Idries Shah, who wrote *The Sufis*, these wandering dervishes were often seen dressed in patchwork robes. Muhammad apparently wore one of these robes as well. The Sufis sewed patches on their robes in a secret manner of which only they were aware. This enabled them to tell if someone in such a garment was an authentic dervish or not.

The early Sufis would often use drama, rather than words, to teach their lessons. Because of their secretive ways, they were considered to be strange by those who did not understand their methods of communication. Some say there may have been a connection between Sufism and the troubadour movement in Spain.

Sufi Orders began to be established during the 12th century. The spiritual teachers of these orders became known as Shaikhs. Probably the most famous of the Sufi Shaikhs is Jelaluddin Rumi, who lived during the thirteenth century. Rumi established the Mevlevi Order of Sufis, better known as the *Whirling Dervishes*. These men did a circular dance, learned from Rumi, which symbolizes the creation process and then the seeker's return to God. (I had hoped to see the *Whirling Dervishes* when I recently visited Turkey but was informed that they are now only allowed to perform on a special holiday each year.)

In addition to being a great teacher, Rumi also became a world-renown Sufi poet after meeting a wandering dervish known as Shams of Tabriz, who apparently transformed his life and brought out the artistic and poetic potential within him. Rumi's writings are full of metaphors. Translations of his poetry may usually be found in the religious section of bookstores, under Sufism. Listed in the reference section of this book, I have included a book which contains a lovely sample of his better-known poems. It is entitled *The Essential Rumi*, translated by Coleman Barks.

Another important figure in Sufism was El-Ghazali, sometimes known during the middle ages in Europe as Algazel. El-Ghazali pointed out the importance of blending the mystical aspects of Sufism with the theological aspects of Islam. He was a dervish who spoke of music as a way of elevating one's consciousness. (See *The Sufis*, by Idries Shah for more information about El-Ghazali.)

Because Sufis tend to focus on the passages in the *Qur'an* which deal with love and mysticism, rather than on strict adherence to Islamic laws, many Fundamental Muslim leaders consider Sufism to be threatening to their belief system and authority. Some Muslims are concerned about the similarity between Sufism and other religions such as those taught by Gnostics, Hindus, and Kabbalists.

Sufism is not well received in much of the Muslim world because it does not outwardly exemplify the more fundamental Islamic practices. For instance, Muslims do not condone music or dancing as part of religious practice. Nor do they believe that reverence for one's teacher or anyone but God, for that matter, should be condoned.

In a similar way that the early Christian Gnostics and Jewish Kabbalists were considered to be heretics, Sufis are considered by many Muslims to be heretics as well. On the other hand, many Sufi leaders consider Sufism to be at the very heart of Islamic teachings. One such leader is Shaykh Fadhlalla Haeri, who wrote *The Elements of Sufism*. Even though he feels Sufism cannot be separated from Islam, he does admit that it has been influenced by Gnostic, Kabbalist, and even Buddhist teachings.

In most Muslim countries, there is no separation between church and state. Islam, therefore, is more than a religion. It is a way of life. In some ways, Muslim women are protected under the law but in other ways, according to western standards, they have no protection at all and are quite unfairly treated. Though there is apparently no mention of veiling women in the *Qur'an,* in many Muslim nations this is strictly enforced. This is not true in all Muslim nations, however. For instance, Turkey has become a secular state. (When I visited Istanbul recently, the woman tour guide was not veiled even when she took our group inside the mosques.)

Carl Ernst, who wrote *Sufism,* tells us that Hazrat Inayat Khan was one of the primary teachers who brought Sufism to the west in the early 20th century. His son, Vilayat Inayat Khan came to America in the 1960's, bringing a version of Sufism which had been combined with some of the practices of other religions, such as Buddhism and Hinduism. He was called Pir Vilayat by his students. "Pir" is a title of respect which students use in referring to their Sufi teachers.

The media in today's world tends to focus a great deal on the animosity which exists between Muslim countries and the West. This, of course, has been exacerbated by the recent terrorist attacks on the United States, which appear to have been caused by terrorists based in Afghanistan. It is more important than ever before to recognize that terrorists are fanatics on the fringe of the Islamic world. They do not in any way represent true Islamic teachings, which are designed to promote peace and harmony in the world, not hatred and violence.

Sufi Practices

Sufis try to remember God through such practices as dhikr (which means to remember). Dhikr is the repetition of God's name. Sufis also pray to God for guidance in their lives. They try to purify their hearts so that this guidance may be felt. In order to do this, they feel that they must face the darker aspects of themselves which have been repressed into the unconscious realm. These unconscious aspects of themselves are often revealed through dreams. Part of the Sufi Path involves working with dreams, often in a group under the direction of a Sufi teacher.

Becoming whole human beings, therefore, is part of the Sufi journey. It involves psychological work on oneself as well as spiritual work. To use alchemy as a metaphor for the process, the Sufi's inner work is like turning lead into gold, or transforming that which was hidden into the light of awareness.

Vaughan-Lee explains in his book, *The Circle of Love,* that, within the Naqshbandi order, friends along the pathway meet together in circles to process their dreams. His teacher, Irina Tweedie, who studied with Bhai Sahib in India, recognized the Sufi dream work was similar to the dream work taught in Jungian Psychology. Jung had referred to the darker aspects of oneself as "the shadow." Once previously disowned qualities have been brought to the surface, according to his teachings, they can be integrated appropriately into the personality.

Idries Shah *(The Sufis)*, emphasizes the importance of finding a teacher if one is serious about following the Sufi Path. The teacher can help students to integrate the various parts of themselves which are revealed to them through dreams. The teacher can also help students to awaken certain energy centers in their bodies, called latifa. These energy centers enable them to develop spiritual powers. It is important for the students to realize, however, that these powers are gifts from God and should be used accordingly. The teacher is there to guide them in this respect. Although Shah indicates that the latifa are different from the chakras of Hinduism, there do seem to be some similarities in their functions.

Sufi teachers often use parables or allegories to teach their students. This is similar to the way in which Jesus taught his disciples. It is also similar to the way that Buddhist teachers use koans (questions which cannot be answered in a rational manner) in order to help their students to learn to rely on their intuition rather than linear reasoning. Sufi teachers are often able to tune in telepathically to their students and to intuitively know what they need to work on in themselves. Students are encouraged to let go of unhealthy habits such as materialism, greed, and laziness. It is important for them to revere and respect their teacher, but, in the end, to become independent of that teacher. In some Sufi orders the teacher's robe (often patched) is passed down to the one who is to become the next teacher of the order.

In Sufi gatherings, poetry and stories are often read. Calligraphy is also shared. Dancing is also done in some circles. We have already discussed the *Whirling Dervishes* and the dance performances that they give. There is also a more informal type of Sufi Dancing which is practiced, particularly in the west. Songs from different spiritual traditions are included to promote world peace. Participants gather in a circle and sing these songs as they move around the circle, dancing with different partners. There are a few musicians who play in the center of the circle as the dancers move around in the circle. Simple instruments, such as a drum and flute, are usually included. As one dances around with different partners, one is encouraged to look each one in the eye and see God's presence there.

In some westernized versions of Sufism in Europe and America, there is not much emphasis on practicing the Islamic faith or even in becoming a dervish. Participants do strive to become closer to God, however. They use chanting, meditation, and dream work to help to purify their hearts. David Cooper writes about Sufism, Buddhism, and Judaism in his book, *Three Gates to Meditation Practice*. In the book he describes the experiences he and his wife, Susan, had while living in a Sufi community in the United States. The people in the community would gather together to practice dhikr as well as meditation, singing, and Sufi Dancing. They would also have healing circles and groups in which dreams were shared and processed for spiritual purposes. Even though Cooper and his wife were Jewish and engaged in Kabbalist practices, they integrated Sufi teachings and practices into lives, as well as Buddhist meditations.

Because it is difficult to describe mystical ecstasy in linear terms, the metaphorical language of poetry is a vehicle which Sufis often use to describe their experiences. One well-known Sufi poet was Omar Khayyam, who lived during the eleventh century. His most famous work is *The Rubaiyat of Omar Khayyam*, also known as *Wine of the Mystic*. Paramahansa Yogananda wrote a beautiful commentary on it, published after his death by the Self Realization Fellowship. There is a deep spiritual interpretation of the work even though it sounds romantic on the surface. Yogananda brings out in his commentaries, for instance, that Sufis use the effects of wine, to represent the idea of becoming "intoxicated" with God's love.

Though some say that the Sufi Path may not be separated from Islam, from which it originated, others say that, because of its mystical nature, it is universal and may be practiced within the framework of almost any religious faith. Though most Sufis live ordinary lives and have families, jobs, etc. they also have rich inner lives and constantly feel the presence of God. They pray for help in developing positive qualities in their lives, such as love and compassion. They also try to let go of outer expectations of how their lives will unfold and to allow the Spirit inside to guide them. In other words, they surrender totally to God.

Concluding Comments

We have seen in our exploration of Sufism that there are many similarities between this path and other mystical approaches to the spiritual journey. For instance, Sufis are similar to Gnostics and Kabbalists, as well as Hindus, in that they aspire to unite with and awaken the Divine aspect of themselves where God resides. Below are some important concepts which stand out as being essential to this spiritual pathway.

Sufis experience a deep longing to return home to God, activated by a voice from within.

There is a deep love for God in the core of the Sufi's heart.

The mystical journey back to God is difficult to describe in linear terms; thus poetry is often used as a vehicle for expression.

Sufism has been referred to as the mystical aspect of Islam but it is also practiced by others who are not of the Islamic faith.

Sufis attempt to purify their hearts in preparation for union with God. There are many tools which help them to do this, including prayer, dream work, and the release of unhealthy life patterns.

A teacher or guide, along the Sufi Path, is important to assist the seeker to stay on the path and to cope with new spiritual insights as they develop.

Union with God, to the Sufi, is a love affair of the highest calling and one which results in a merging of one's essence or "light" with God's essence or "light" and allowing this "light upon light" to extend out into the world.

Personal Reflections

As a psychologist, I appreciate the psycho-spiritual inner work which takes place along the Sufi Path. I also enjoy some of its other practices, such as Sufi Dancing. I remember when a friend took me to an old church building on a Friday night where people in beautiful, flowing clothes were gathered together. We all took our shoes off and made a circle. In the center of the circle were a few musicians, who had brought their drums, flute, and keyboard. The circle was opened by our leader, who led us in the recitation of a beautiful prayer, entitled "Toward the One." The essence was that, no matter who we were or where we came from, we were all headed toward the One Creator of us all. The beginning prayer touched me deeply and helped me to feel very connected to this group of people even though I was new to the Sufi experience.

I still go to Sufi Dance circles upon occasion. We are instructed to turn toward a partner, either right or left, until everyone has found someone to team up with. One of the musicians is usually prepared to join the circle in case another dance partner is needed. We are then taught a short song of praise, along with some simple movements to do with our partner. We are reminded to smile and look each other in the eyes, "seeing" the light of God in each face. After doing this once, we progress to the next partner and repeat the song and movements again. This continues until we have gone full circle. Then another song is taught and we dance again. After a number of songs and dances are completed, we all participate in a meditation, closing song, and the chanting of AUM. Then there are announcements and a closing prayer. After each Sufi Dance experience, I find that the songs continue to play in my mind (even into my dreams at times).

I don't remember exactly when it happened for me, but on one very special night, while Sufi Dancing, I had a strange and wonderful sensation that everyone in the circle was an angel. It was an experience which I shall never forget (one in which something ordinary was suddenly transformed into something extraordinarily beautiful).

If you travel this pathway, you may find that some form of creative expression is necessary in order to describe the mystical experiences which you may have. Since poetry has been my creative medium, I am particularly attracted to the use of poetry in Sufism.

As mentioned in Chapter Six, there were some similarities which I noted between the Kabbalah Story of Creation and one the *Squnch* stories, written by Barbara Morse. It is interesting that I also discovered a similarity between a character in Morse's stories, called the *Sqump,* and the Sufi wandering dervishes. The *Sqump* had apparently stopped talking because people did not understand what he was trying to communicate. He, therefore, used mime, drama, and art in order to get across his messages. He also carried his belongings around in a patchwork quilt. (The wandering dervishes, of course, wore patchwork cloaks and communicated through drama.)

I asked Barbara Morse if she had been exposed to Sufism before writing the stories and she said that she had not. She was just as amazed as I was at the interesting similarity I had found. I believe that she had somehow touched into a universal pool of images and symbols when writing her stories. Once again, we have an example of how astonishing the creative process really is.

Practice Exercises

Sufi Dancing

Check out the Internet or New Age periodicals to see if Sufi Dancing is offered near you. It is a wonderful experience and I highly recommend it. As you dance, remember to look at each person as if he or she is an expression of the Divine.

Dreams

Begin a dream journal. Think of each aspect of your dreams as an aspect of yourself and allow the different parts to dialog with each other. Join a dream group if possible.

Working With Your Shadow

See if you can think of the many parts within yourself which vie for attention (such as the studious one, the child-like one, the mother, etc.). Write them down. Then allow these parts to talk with each other (in your mind) to identify what they want and need from you. Acknowledge each one and try to think of ways to meet their needs.

Poetry

After a period of meditation or communing with nature, sit with a paper and pen and allow words to flow through you onto the paper. See what kind of poetry comes through you in this manner. If you are an artist, allow a painting or drawing to come forth.

Releasing Old Patterns

Spend a day looking at your life as if it is a drama. See if you can observe patterns which are healthy and patterns which are not. Resolve to let go of some of the unhealthy patterns which no longer serve you.

Learning New Lessons

If you find yourself getting emotionally upset by an event in your life, explore where in your psyche that feeling comes from. It may be something which you repressed in your life and projected onto someone else. Think in terms of looking at the "mirrors" which other people hold up for you so that you can learn more about yourself.

Chapter Eight
New Thought
Movement

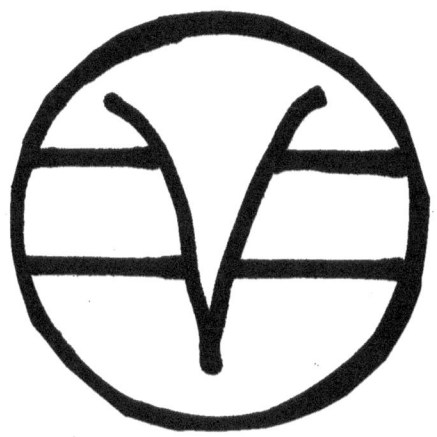

Along the path of the New Thought Movement, we learn that the Divine Spirit is omnipresent (existing everywhere at all times in all things). In the symbol above (from the Church of Religious Science), the "V" represents this omnipresence, reaching downward through: (1) The Realm of the Creator, (2) The Law of Creation, and (3) The Realm of the Created. As we awaken to that which is divine within us, we can help to bring qualities, such as love, peace, and harmony into the world.

New Thought Movement

Introduction

Many people confuse the term, New Thought, with New Age. Though there may be an overlap in some of the thinking of New Age and New Thought adherents, the two movements are basically very different. New Age refers to the current time in our history when people on our planet are becoming more receptive to exploring the non-physical, or occult, world. For example, under the New Age umbrella, one may study such things as numerology, astrology, crystals, and tarot. Some study for spiritual reasons and others simply out of curiosity. On the other hand, the New Thought Movement is a specific pathway in which one's mental processes are closely linked to the application of spiritual principles.

The New Thought Movement arose in the United States of America during the latter part of the 19th century. Its concepts were not really new. In fact, many of them were similar to those of three other spiritual movements in the United States at that time. These include Transcendentalism, Spiritualism, and Theosophy. Transcendentalism was being practiced in New England and had arisen as an alternative to a more traditional form of Christianity. Transcendentalists were seeking opportunities to approach God directly through their inner experiences. Spiritualism is a metaphysical (beyond physical) philosophy which focuses on communicating with the spirits of those who have died. Theosophy blends mystical ideas from Hinduism, Buddhism, and some of the mystery religions from ancient times, with more recent western philosophies.

The New Thought Movement, probably more akin to Transcendentalism than to the other two philosophies, uses rational, as well as mystical, explanations to explain metaphysics.

148

Pioneers in the Movement

One of the most famous Transcendentalists was Ralph Waldo Emerson. He taught and wrote that, by improving one's thinking, one may learn to create a more positive life experience. In his essay, The Over-Soul, found in a book entitled, *Emerson's Essays*, he describes a spiritual presence which he believed surrounds all human beings. According to Emerson, it is the individual soul, or core being of an individual, through which the Over-Soul, or Divine is revealed. He also suggests that enlightenment is possible when one pays attention to the universal truths revealed in this manner. This is similar to the "Atman" concept in Hinduism (described in Chapter Three).

The Transcendentalists distinguished between the Infinite God and finite matter. They taught that human beings, by recognizing their unity with the Infinite God, may begin to release fear and embrace love more fully in their lives. A similar teaching is found in the *Course in Miracles* (described in Chapter Six).

Some people refer to Ralph Waldo Emerson as the Father of New Thought because he highlighted many of the concepts which were later incorporated into the movement. One concept is that the power of one's thoughts may be utilized in such a way as to actually bring into physical manifestation that which one desires. Another is the notion that Jesus Christ came to the world, not to be worshipped, but to teach people how to live their lives as spiritual beings. Transcendentalists wanted to emulate Jesus and practice his teachings on their own, rather than under the authority of an organized religious institution.

Charles Braden, in his book, *Spirits in Rebellion*, emphasizes how leaders in the New Thought Movement expanded the ideas of others who had come

149

before them. For instance, an English judge by the name of Thomas Troward organized Emerson's ideas into a logical format. Some of Troward's ideas also came from eastern religions. During the latter part of the 19th century, he had been sent by the Queen of England to serve as a judge in Punjab, India. During his time there, he studied eastern mystical practices and compared them with Emerson's ideas and some of his own spiritual beliefs. At Edinburgh, Scotland and then at the Dore' gallery in London, he presented many of these ideas to very receptive audiences. Troward's lectures have been compiled in a book entitled, *The Edinburgh & Dore' Lectures on Mental Science.*

Just as Emerson had a great influence on Troward, Troward, in turn, had a great influence on the American New Thought leader, Ernest Holmes. Holmes incorporated many of Troward's ideas into his own book, *The Science of Mind*, published in 1927. Holmes also started the *Science of Mind* magazine and, with his brother, Fenwicke, established an institute to promote New Thought teachings. In 1967 this institute evolved into a religious organization called *The International Association of Religious Science Churches.* Since then, several branches of Religious Science Churches have developed. In addition there are some independent Science of Mind churches in existence today. The newest branch of Religious Science focuses on the healing of the planet and is called *Global Religious Science Ministries.*

Like Emerson, Phineas Quimby is also referred to as the Father of New Thought. Quimby was born around the same time as Emerson in the early 1800's. Whereas Emerson was primarily a philosopher and minister, Quimby, on the other hand, was part of the New Thought Movement because of his use of mental and spiritual means in the healing process. Many of his teachings were compiled by Mason Clark in a book entitled, *The Healing Wisdom of Dr. P. P. Quimby.*

Quimby claimed to "see" the spirits of his patients. He would ask the spirits to explain what was causing the symptoms in his patients. In response, the spirits would supposedly outline for him the negative thought patterns which his patients needed to release in order to be healed.

Many people went to Quimby for healing and also to learn how to apply his procedures. He reported that his methods were modeled after those used by Jesus in biblical days. Quimby taught his students that their thoughts could be picked up psychically by others. In order to explain this, he used mothers as an example, suggesting that their negative thoughts could be picked up by their children and subsequently result in the symptoms of an illness. When the mothers' thoughts were changed into positive ones, he suggested, the symptoms in their children would disappear. Reportedly, Quimby's methods were put to the test successfully by many mothers who came to him for assistance.

Phineas Quimby healed some people who went on to establish New Thought Churches One of them was Mary Baker Eddy, who founded the Christian Science Church. Eventually, this church became separated from the rest of the New Thought Movement because of a basic difference in philosophy. In Christian Science, only the spiritual is considered to be real. Matter, on the other hand, is viewed as unreal or illusory. Because of this, medical treatments, which are in the realm of matter, are not endorsed by Christian Science followers. Only prayer is considered to be an appropriate treatment for illnesses. New Thought healers do not view matter as being unreal, but rather as a transient condition or effect. Spirit, on the other hand, is viewed as eternal. Under this system of thought, medical treatments may be used to address the temporary conditions of the body, while prayer is used to address spiritual needs (thought to have been responsible for the symptoms in the first place).

Another important New Thought teacher during the late 1800's, early 1900's, was Emma Curtis Hopkins. She started out as editor of the Christian Science Journal and then left Christian Science to teach New Thought principles in her own way, establishing a seminary in Chicago where students could study and become ordained as ministers. In her book, *Scientific Christian Mental Practice*, Hopkins describes important New Thought principles. She was another pioneer who applied the teachings of Jesus in her own life and taught that this could be done by anyone who intended to do so. One of her primary teachings was that God's creations are basically good. According to her way of thinking, even if outer circumstances seem negative, it is important to view them as necessary for one's growth and well-being. Hopkins also taught her students to write down their affirmations in order to empower the oral with the written word. Like others before her, she stressed the power of love in the healing process.

Hopkins became a teacher of several students who later established New Thought organizations and churches or taught others who went on to do so. For instance, Charles and Myrtle Fillmore, both students of Hopkins, later founded the Unity School of Christianity. In addition, Ernest Holmes, who later founded the Church of Religious Science, was a student of Hopkins at one time.

Another pioneer in the New Thought Movement was Ralph Waldo Trine. In his book, *In Tune With The Infinite*, first published in 1899, Trine suggested that there is a connection among all of the religions of the world and that God is present within everyone. Trine spoke out against the idea of converting people to a particular spiritual path and pointed out that there are many ways to approach God. He also wrote that the thoughts one has around his or her pets may actually bring about positive or negative behaviors in them. There are people in today's society who study animal behavior and adhere to a similar principle in teaching pet owners how to communicate more effectively with their animals. Trine's teachings regarding animal communication are similar to Quimby's teachings regarding communication between mothers and their children.

Principles and Practices

In discussing the basic spiritual principles and practices generally associated with the New Thought Movement, we are focusing primarily on the teachings of Ernest Holmes. His book, *The Science of Mind*, having been revised several times, is one of the most popular texts of the New Thought Movement. I have chosen to highlight it because it represents a synthesis of ideas from various New Thought pioneers, integrated with eastern mystical teachings.

Holmes brought forth three basic concepts which seem to be important to those on the New Thought path. One is the idea that there is an Infinite Spirit which created the universe and which permeates everything in it. The second is that human beings, being created in the image of the Infinite Spirit, are manifestations of Spirit in the physical world. The third concept has to do with the creation process itself. According to Science of Mind principles, the creative aspect of Infinite Spirit is referred to as the Universal Law. It works automatically in the universe to bring forth that which Infinite Spirit chooses to bring forth. Since we, as human beings are manifestations of Spirit in the physical world, we may create as well. Our subconscious minds work like the Universal Law. Whatever they are fed, they bring about. Sometimes we are out of touch with negative motivations or mind-sets (brought about by painful experiences from the past), which have gotten stuck in our subconscious minds. Even though we want to bring about positive changes in our lives, these negative attitudes sabotage

153

the process. When we align ourselves with Infinite Spirit, we are asking for assistance in releasing negative attitudes so that the outcomes we want may be brought about.

A specific tool, referred to as Spiritual Mind Treatment, is taught in the Church of Religious Science. It is an affirmative type of prayer which includes five basic steps, each associated with a kind of inner or outer statement which one makes during the treatment. When I took the foundation class in Science of Mind principles, we were taught to remember the steps in Spiritual Mind Treatment with the code, "Are (R) you (U) ready (R) to receive (R)?" These letters actually stand for the steps of Recognition, Union, Realization, Thanks, and Release.

Under the first step in a Spiritual Mind Treatment, *recognition,* a statement is made which recognizes God or the Infinite Spirit as being Omnipresent. In the second step, *union,* a statement is made which supports the notion that all human beings are unified with God. This gives us the opportunity to express God-like qualities in our lives if we choose to do so. In the third step, *realization,* a statement is made which suggests that the treatment goals have already been realized in a spiritual sense. The next step, *thanks,* involves making a statement of gratitude. This is an important aspect of the treatment simply because it is an appropriate response when a gift has been given. It is also a way of suggesting that the treatment has been successful. The last step, *release,* involves releasing the treatment into Universal Law for manifestation in the physical realm.

The more faith or belief a person has that the Infinite Spirit is present in the co-creation process, the more power Spiritual Mind Treatments have. An interesting juxtaposition of attitudes takes place in that one *puts forth* an intention while, at the same time, *surrendering* to Spirit, having faith that whatever comes will be the gift which is needed. Spirit sometimes brings forth situations in which deeper unconscious attitudes may be identified

154

and released. This paves the way for more positive outcomes to show up when one is truly ready to welcome them into his or her life.

Rev. Dr. Christian Sorensen, who so graciously wrote the foreword to this book, is the head minister at *Seaside Church of Religious Science*, located in Encinitas, California. He includes, in all of his services, a prayer in the form of a Spiritual Mind Treatment. In these prayers, or treatments, he often offers healing words for people in the church who may be experiencing serious illnesses, deaths, or other challenges in their lives. His words are spoken in a way to remind them that Spirit is present in the midst of their difficulties and that they will come through the experience in a positive manner. Rev. Christian also enjoys surfing and flying airplanes. In his books, *Catch the Spirit: Riding the Waves of Life* and *Catch the Spirit: Flying Through Life,* he does a beautiful job of using the metaphors of surfing and flying to explain Science of Mind principles. For instance, using the metaphor of free-falling into a wave and joyfully becoming one with it, he talks about surrendering to the awareness that one is unified with the Spirit Within. Likewise, using the metaphor of flying, he talks about such things as letting go of excess baggage in one's life, going on an inner journey, and fueling one's life with love. His books are not only fun to read but are very instructive as well.

Unity is another church which teaches New Thought principles. Founded in Kansas City, Missouri, by Charles and Myrtle Fillmore, its headquarters still remain in that area. The Fillmores, who once studied with Emma Curtis Hopkins, taught that God is not a person or entity, but may be considered, instead, to be the Spirit of Truth which reveals itself to those who are open to receiving instruction from within. The Fillmores used prayer circles and classes to assist their students in becoming receptive to this kind of inner guidance.

Unity churches are very similar to Religious Science churches in that God is viewed as a Source of Divine Energy which may be found within oneself. In Unity, there is also a strong emphasis on applying the teachings and healing methods brought to the world by Jesus Christ. Unlike traditional Christian churches, Unity participants strive to follow Jesus's example by applying his healing methods and teachings to their everyday lives rather than focusing on worshiping him as a deity. This practical application of spiritual principles is what makes Unity a part of the New Thought Movement.

The Divine Science Church is also considered to be a part of the New Thought Movement. Its headquarters are located in Denver, Colorado. It was founded by Nona Brooks and Melinda Cramer, both of whom had been healed by spiritual means. Divine Science teachings are very similar to those of Religious Science and Unity. By aligning one's individual mind with the Universal Mind, it is taught that one may unite mystically with the Divine Presence. Healing is the natural result of such a union.

Agape, located in Los Angeles, California, is a New Thought church headed by Dr. Michael Beckwith. *Agape* is well known, among other things, for its wonderful musical ministry. A few years ago, Dr. Beckwith visited Accra, Ghana in Africa, and was interested in finding out if there were any New Thought churches there. He was pointed in the direction of an organization called *The Etherean Mission Application Technology* (EMAT). Brother Ishmael Tetteh, an African mystic, had founded the organization for the purpose of liberating people from the adverse effects of negative thought patterns. He had been teaching scientific spiritual principles long before he ever heard of the New Thought Movement in the United States. Tetteh writes in some of his publications that he intuitively knew that someone from the West would be instrumental in furthering the teachings of EMAT.

When Beckwith arrived in Ghana, Tetteh "knew" that Beckwith was the person he was destined to meet. Since that time, Tetteh has been coming to the United States at least once a year to speak to the congregation at *Agape*. He has also made connections with the *Seaside Church of Religious Science* in Encinitas, CA, which is how I came to know and study with him.

One of the most powerful techniques for liberation taught by EMAT is called Soul Processing. By using this process, one not only works with changing conscious thought patterns, but goes even deeper by addressing negative thoughts associated with painful memories trapped in the unconscious or subconscious mind. A person using this technique (the liberatee) identifies painful memories in his or her life. He or she then processes these memories by "reliving" them (describing them as if they were happening in present time) under the guidance of a trained partner (the liberator). After going over these events several times and releasing the negative emotions associated with them, a special "lesson" or "learning" is identified and named. This reframes the painful memory in a positive light.

By clearing out negative thought patterns from the past, one eliminates "triggers" which bring about apathy, anger, fear, or other negative feelings in one's daily life, thus making it possible for more positive feelings, such as peace, joy, and love, to be activated. Special techniques are utilized in Soul Processing in order to recapture and release the negative emotions associated with early memories. Once this has been done, energy which had been stuck in the past is brought into present time for a more constructive purposes.

Another goal of Soul Processing is to help individuals to discover what Tetteh describes as the "God Qualities" in themselves so that their lives may be lived on the highest level of consciousness possible. This helps them to fulfill whatever purpose they came to earth to fulfill. Like Science of Mind, EMAT teaches that evil is simply a misuse of Universal Law. In other words, when one's thoughts are of a destructive nature, evil is the result. When one's thoughts are of a constructive nature, good is the result. If interested in more details regarding Soul Processing, be sure to read *The Etherean Mission Application Technology, 2nd Edition*, by Brother Ishmael N.O. Tetteh, listed in the reference section.

Related Metaphysical Teachings

There are many systems of thought in existence today, some ancient and others more contemporary, which complement the New Thought Movement. One author, who is also a teacher of "contemporary mysticism," is Dr. Caroline Myss. Her book, *Anatomy of the Spirit: The Seven Stages of Power and Healing*, has already been mentioned in the chapter on Hinduism. Myss describes herself as a medical intuitive (one who can "see" illnesses in people). In her work, she has discovered that illness is most often caused by one's attachment to wounds or pains received in the past. By releasing these attachments, according to Myss, one can bring the energy (which has been used to keep those wounds alive) back to present time for more constructive purposes. This is very similar to the Soul Processing techniques taught by Brother Ishmael Tetteh.

Another contemporary teacher in the United States today is Terry Livingood, who wrote *The Bible for Translating from Physical to Spirit*. This is a beautiful guidebook which may be used to assist in awakening the spiritual essence of one's being. Based on the teachings of Jesus and other spiritual masters, Livingood's bible may be read from beginning to end or at random. It is filled with inspirational passages meant to be read in the present tense, as if the reader has already mastered its teachings. This is similar to the New Thought philosophy of stating one's desires as if they have already been manifested. There are references taken from the more familiar Christian

Bible as well as other verses, written by the Livingood, which have been included to expand upon various themes.

Originally meant to be a personal guidebook for himself, Livingood's bible was eventually published at the request of his friends, who insisted that it would be useful for anyone on a spiritual path. It is stressed that human beings, following Jesus's example, may overcome death by learning to "translate" from physical matter into spiritual essence. The bible is a tool to assist in this process. Just as Jesus was a master of life, Livingood's belief is that ordinary people can, likewise, learn to be masters.

One of the ancient metaphysical philosophies which complements the New Thought Movement is African mysticism. Brother Ishmael N.O. Tetteh has written a book about the subject, entitled, *The Inspired African Mystical Gospel, Vol. 1 (IAM Gospel)*. In this book, he discusses a desire to bring back into public awareness the African mysticism which was practiced freely before colonial powers gained control of the native Africans, forcing other religions, such as Christianity, upon them. He believes that ancient African religions can help human beings learn to live more harmoniously with nature. To the African, the earth is considered to be the female aspect of God. Both the female and male aspects of God and of human beings, are honored. In addition, Tetteh feels that there is a need to heal the African Spirit which was damaged by so many years of enslavement. By bringing African mysticism to the public eye, he hopes to address this need and empower modern Africans.

Tetteh also points out how New Thought philosophies may be blended effectively with ancient African religious belief systems. Like New Thought philosophies (which teach that there is divinity within), the African religions teach that even the individual cells in our bodies are divine in nature. The "spirit" or "god" of each organ, therefore, may be called upon to help in the healing process.

Like Native Americans (described in Chapter One), Africans use stories, songs, and dances to communicate their beliefs. In Ghana, they bring the Divine into a personal realm by referring to God as Onyankupon, which means Big Friend. Within the African religions, gods and goddesses are viewed as God's emissaries (much as angels are viewed in Christianity).

Concluding Comments

We have discussed many New Thought ideas and related teachings in this chapter. The following list includes some of the most prevalent and important ideas which are representative of this spiritual pathway.

In addition to being viewed as Creator, the Infinite Spirit is also viewed as Omnipresent (permeating the entire universe with its essence.)

One aspect of the Infinite Spirit is the Universal Law of Creation (the process by which creation occurs.)

Human beings are viewed as manifestations of the Infinite Spirit in the physical world.

Negative thought patterns, often associated with pains from the past, tend to bring about negative circumstances in life. By the same token, positive thought patterns tend to bring about positive circumstances.

If a person freely chooses to align his or her mind with the Infinite Spirit, the Universal Law of Creation works with all layers of that person's mind (conscious, subconscious, and unconscious) in order to facilitate the bringing about of positive circumstances.

One's physical body is viewed as real, but transient, whereas one's spirit is viewed as eternal and the essence of one's being.

> *By aligning the individual mind with the Mind of God, one*
> *may assist in the co-creation of a world in which it is*
> *possible for love, peace and harmony to prevail.*

Personal Reflections

I have been very fortunate to attend the *Seaside Church of Religious Science* for the past seven years. I enjoy Rev. Christian's uplifting messages, as well as the wonderful music, which expresses New Thought ideas in a beautiful and moving manner. I have also taken advantage of some of the Science of Mind classes available at the church.

By utilizing Spiritual Mind Treatments, I have been able to cooperate with Spirit in manifesting many things in my life. For instance, since childhood, I had always wanted to visit Greece. It seemed to me that it was my destiny to go their someday. I decided to focus on this in my prayer treatments. To emphasize my intention in a visual way, I decided, with the help of Batya, an artist friend of mine, to make some place-mats with beautiful pictures of Greece on them. I put these place-mats out on the table each night and marveled at the beauty of the Greek Isles. This was a way of instructing my subconscious mind (and letting the Universal Law know) that it was my intention to go there. It was amazing to me that, within a year, my husband and I were spending our honeymoon on a cruise ship in the Greek Islands.

I have also been fortunate in attending a Soul Processing class, taught by Brother Ishmael Tetteh, the African mystic described earlier. I found Soul Processing to be an extremely powerful technique to quickly and effectively get to the core of many of the negative triggers in my life, associated with painful memories. By processing these memories, I was able to reduce (and in some cases, release) the pain associated with them. For instance, by reliving the events associated with my father's suicide, I was able to recognize that some of my depressive tendencies were subconsciously "picked up" from my father. By recognizing this, I was in a better position to separate his attitudes from my own and to, consequently, release negative thought patterns which no longer served my life in a constructive manner.

In addition to the work which I have done on myself, using Science of Mind and Soul Processing principles, I have also experienced some synchronistic events since beginning work on this chapter. For instance, I was recently exposed to Terry Livingood's book, *The Bible for Translating from Physical to Spirit*, through a friend of our family, George Emery. Emery is a minister who lives in a spiritual community known as *Sunrise Ranch* in Loveland, Colorado. Livingood had given him ten autographed books to be distributed among his friends and I happened to be one of the lucky recipients. This book has enhanced my own spiritual journey immensely and I highly recommend it. It is included in the reference section in case you are interested in obtaining a copy. I might also add that *Sunrise Ranch* is a model community where people have learned to live together in harmony, each contributing in their own unique way to the good of the group. Emery and the other people who live at *Sunrise Ranch* refer to themselves as emissaries of the Divine Presence, promoting love and peace in the world.

Another synchronistic event occurred when I was speaking with my sister, Dianne, on the phone. She said that she had been cleaning out some of her closets and happened upon an old book entitled, *In Tune With the Infinite*, by Ralph Waldo Trine. I had never heard of Trine before, but we were both astonished as to how similar his words were to the words of New Thought teachers in today's world. I later came upon a more recent publication of the same work. Finding it to be a good resource for New Thought, I included a discussion of it in this chapter.

Synchronistic events are examples of how Spirit can work in ones's life, when invited to do so. Of course, when Spirit is in the lead, things often happen in a different fashion than expected. In addition, the time line may be different. Science of Mind teaches that it is important to release one's will to the a higher consciousness and to trust that whatever happens will be for one's highest good. This teaching has helped me to get through some of the difficult challenges that have presented themselves in my life.

Within the New Thought Movement, it is stressed that there are many pathways to God. Pathways congruent with New Thought teach that the Divine Presence actually exists within each human being on earth. Therefore, no one is left out. This is the kind of teaching which I respect and am able to accept as part of my own spiritual journey. It allows me to continue with practices which I have come to rely upon from the other spiritual pathways discussed in this book, while also viewing them within the framework of New Thought principles.

The following exercises are included to give you a chance to experience some of the principles of the New Thought Movement for yourself.

Practice Exercises

Watch your thoughts

Pay attention during the course of a day to the thoughts of your mind. Note negative as well as positive thoughts. At the end of the day, write a page in your journal, describing your thoughts and what happened as a result of them. Keep this journal for at least a month and review it to see if patterns emerge. Make modifications accordingly.

Search for memories

When negative thoughts or pains arise in your life, think back to the earliest times when you thought or felt that way. This may give you a clue as to the root of some of your present-day problems.

Make affirmations

Begin to write and state positive affirmations about the goals you want to achieve in life. Write them as though they have already been achieved. Place them around your home so that they can be reminders of what you are attempting to bring about. Remember that aligning your affirmations with the Spirit Within will help you to co-create a beautiful life for yourself and others.

Express yourself artistically

Create a collage of those things in life which you would like to manifest. This is a tangible way of letting the universe know what your intentions are.

Ask for Healing

When you experience physical pain, ask the spirit of the part of your body, where the pain is located, to reveal to you what the pain represents.

Some of Louise Hay's books on healing may also be used. Hay has done a lot of research in this area and has associated specific bodily pains with specific negative thought patterns. (See references.)

Co-create with God

Take time to see God in every aspect of your world, even in yourself. Begin to explore ways of manifesting positive qualities of the Divine in your life. Think of yourself as "God expressing in the world," creating a positive framework which can be spiritually empowering.

Express gratitude

Don't forget to express gratitude every single day for the wonderful things in life which Spirit manifests through you. In addition, be ready to release negative thought patterns no longer serving your life in a constructive manner.

Pamela Allen

Conclusion

Conclusion

By writing this book, it was my desire to contribute to a better understanding among people from various ethnic and religious groups. The themes emerging from this research suggest that it is possible for diverse spiritual groups to co-exist in peace and harmony. If the more traditional religions of the world can learn to accept and appreciate each other in a similar way, perhaps peace will be possible on our planet.

On a more personal level, I wanted to provide some tools which people could use to gain more understanding, peace and harmony within themselves. All of us struggle from time to time from the wars which go on within us as we try to make sense out of our lives. I have found, within the paths explored in this book, some tools which have helped to free me from some of my own inner struggles and which may prove to be liberating for you as well. I consider these to be gifts from Spirit. They are presented for you in the second section of this chapter, along with suggestions as to how to open up to your own inner guidance.

Basic Themes

Based on the eight sacred paths we have explored, there are seven basic themes which have emerged. They may be described metaphorically as colorful threads which make up a sacred tapestry. Some interconnect while others seem to form unique designs which complement one another.

> *Theme #1: There are many paths to that which is Divine. Teachings from one path often overlap with teachings from another.*

There are many paths available to people who are seeking a spiritual direction in their lives. We have explored only eight. I was drawn to these particular paths because they are not exclusive in their views and promote the idea that spirituality is a personal matter, unrelated to one's religious affiliation. In this respect, they may be called spiritual, rather than religious. That is not to say that one could not have a mystical experience of the Divine within a traditional religious setting. It is to say, however, that the paths included in this book tend to focus more on internal spiritual work than on following the rules and regulations of particular religious organizations.

While doing the research for this book, it was very exciting for me to discover so many similarities among the various pathways. For example, Native Americans, African mystics, and Taoists all stress the importance of living one's life in harmony with nature. All offer tools for aligning oneself with nature and for showing respect and appreciation for everything in life.

I also discovered many similarities between the teachings of Buddha and those of Jesus. For example, both taught the importance of compassion and love in the spiritual paths they presented. Some speculate that Jesus may have visited India and had exposure to Buddhism and Hinduism before his ministry. Others suggest that, since the teachings of both Jesus and Buddha stemmed from their connection with the Divine Presence, it is understandable that the truths flowing through them would be the similar.

It was also interesting for me to discover that the mystical teachings of Gnosticism, Kabbalah, and Sufism are so similar. All three movements, in the beginning, were considered to be heretical in nature because their teachings were against prevailing religious beliefs (Christianity, Judaism, and Islam). More specifically, all promoted the concept that individuals do not have to follow the precepts of traditional religious organizations in order to have direct and personal experiences of the Divine.

I discovered another interesting similarity between New Thought and Kabbalist ideas. When practicing New Thought principles, one may bring forth an intention to manifest something in life. At the same time, however, one must be able to surrender the outcome to Spirit. In a similar way, Kabbalists, working with the Tree of Life, must learn how to balance and harmonize the qualities of persistence (Netzach) with surrender (Hod) if they want to achieve a stable foundation in their lives (Yesod).

An integral part of all the paths we have explored is the idea that no one path is right for everyone. Within each path, there is respect and appreciation for other spiritual traditions. Hinduism, for example, reminds us that different spiritual paths appeal to different people, depending on their dispositions, interests and talents.

Theme #2: A Divine Presence permeates the universe and forms the essence of All That Is.

In weaving a tapestry from the threads of our eight sacred paths, we notice a golden thread which appears to hold them all together and to form a foundation for the other threads and designs. This golden thread, which represents a Divine Presence permeating every aspect of the universe, has been called by many names. Native Americans refer to it as Great Spirit (Wakan Tanka in Lakota). Similarly, African mystics in Ghana refer to it as Onyankupon, which means Big Friend. Taoists refer to it as the Tao, which means The Way.

In order to describe the Divine Presence as a Source, Kabbalists use the term, Ein Sof, which means Nothingness. Out of this Nothingness, ten Sefirot came forth. These Sefirot illustrate qualities of the Divine which are represented in the Kabbalist Tree of Life. Buddhists may refer to the Divine as Nothing At All, and, at the same time, All That Is.

Hindus use many names to describe the Divine Presence, each referring to different qualities. These names include Brahma, Vishnu, Shiva, and Divine Mother. Jesus also used many names to describe the Divine Presence, but seemed to prefer the personal and familiar term, Our Father. Those who follow the *Course in Miracles* refer to it as The Holy Spirit. Sufis refer to it lovingly and intimately as Friend or Beloved.

New Thought adherents tend to use such terms as Father/Mother God, Infinite Spirit, or Spirit in referring to the Divine Presence. They might also make statements such as "God is all there is and there is only God," in referring to this all-pervasive notion of the Divine Presence which permeates everything and everyone.

> *Theme #3: It is possible for us, as human beings, to awaken to the Divine Presence within ourselves. Within each of the eight paths, there are different ways of facilitating this process.*

If the Divine Presence forms the essence of who we are as human beings, then it follows that we are indeed spiritual beings. Awakening to the Spirit Within allows us to feel connected to something greater than ourselves, indeed, something vast and eternal. Awakening to our spiritual nature enables us to bring a sense of that which is sacred into the physical realm in which we live.

Within all eight paths, there are tools which are suggested to awaken us to the Spirit Within. Native Americans use ceremonies such as sweat lodges, medicine wheels, and vision quests to connect themselves to this spiritual energy which they also see manifested in every aspect of nature. Taoists use exercises such as Tai Chi Chuan to center themselves so that ch'i (life energy) from the Tao may flow freely through their bodies and their lives. This ch'i is said to promote a sense of well-being and longevity. When it is blocked, such procedures as acupuncture or Qi-Gong Therapy are used to open up the channels once more so that healing may naturally occur. Hindus, on the other hand, use Hatha Yoga to encourage the flow of prana. Both ch'i and prana refer to life energy, which is believed by Taoists and Hindus alike to be essential for good health and longevity.

Hindus use the term, Atman, to describe an individualized realization of the Divine Presence in a human being who has become awakened to his or her true nature. Buddhists refer to this awakened state of mind as Nirvana, or Heaven on Earth. The name, Buddha, actually means The Awakened One. Jesus, too, is said to have awakened to his divinity. For that reason, he was called Christ. Many people who follow Jesus's teachings today speak of awakening to the Christ Within. Jesus taught his followers that, by loving God and each other, they could connect with the Kingdom of God, which was to be found within themselves.

Kabbalists meditate upon the Tree of Life in an effort to activate Ein Sof's divine qualities within their own lives. Sufis seek to purify their hearts so that the Beloved may take over their lives and live through them. They use poetry and metaphors to describe the blissful state of being united with this Divine Presence. New Thought adherents use affirmative prayers, sometimes known as Spiritual Mind Treatments, to align themselves with this Presence so that it may be expressed lovingly through their lives.

Theme #4: Everything and everyone in the universe is connected by the Divine Presence and each has a purpose and reason for being.

Accepting the idea that everything is connected by the Divine Presence leads to the conclusion that each aspect of the plant, animal, and mineral kingdoms has a vital purpose for being. Native Americans, African mystics, and other indigenous people around the world understand that we, as humans, are part of something bigger and more inclusive than just our species. They remind us that all of nature is sacred and deserving of appreciation, respect, and honor. With our technological advancements, we have sought for years to conquer (rather than to live in harmony with) nature. For this reason, we have caused a great deal of damage to the very earth which sustains our physical life. Out of respect for the physical universe, Native Americans often use familiar, human titles when referring to various aspects of nature (Father Sky, Sister Moon, and Stone People). Taoists also speak of nature as being a teacher, mirroring qualities in human beings which need to be recognized.

Accepting the idea of the interconnection of all things in the universe leads to the conclusion that human beings, regardless of race, gender, or faith, are all part of the same sacred circle of life, each spiritual in his or her essence and worthy of appreciation, respect, and honor. Buddhists recognize this when they point out that, when one being suffers, all suffer. On the other hand, when one shows compassion, all benefit. For this reason, Buddha taught his followers to develop hearts of compassion so that a better world could be created. Like Buddhists, Kabbalists recognize the connection which all beings have with one another and emphasize the importance of showing compassion to those in need. They describe this as a way of "raising the sparks" of divinity.

Jesus taught his followers to love God with all their hearts and to love each other as they love themselves. This implies that everyone (rich or poor, male or female, young or old) is worthy of love. Jesus also taught that, to judge others is to judge oneself and, to help others, is to help oneself.

Sufis teach that the Beloved is everything and that nothing else matters. In Sufi Dancing, they see the Beloved in the faces of everyone in the circle. Within the Course in Miracles as well as in the New Thought Movement, it is taught that, what we give out comes back to us. By loving others, we are also loving ourselves and, by hating others, we are hating ourselves. This is based on the principle that we are all one. What we do to others, we, therefore, do to ourselves. By the same token, what we do to ourselves, we also do to others. It works both ways.

Buddhists remind us of the bliss that results from the feeling of being connected to All That Is. In addition, the Native American Medicine Wheel beautifully depicts the sacred interconnection in life, in which everything fills an important space. If we can truly learn to accept this truth, there will be no more need for wars on our planet, for no one will be judged. There will be no need to place greater value on one person or species over another. All will be seen as integral parts of one another, each with gifts to bring to the grand scheme of things. This is similar to the way in which all the organs in a body work together for the good of that body.

Theme #5: The Divine Presence flows through apparent polarities in the physical universe. Honoring these polarities and balancing them out in our lives allows us, as human beings, to be "in the flow" of the universe.

The yin/yang symbol of Taoism is a beautiful example of how the polarities in life are all part of the whole. Everything in the physical world appears to have a dual nature, which the Taoists describe as either feminine or masculine. There is night and there is day. There is up and there is down. We breathe in and we breathe out. In the yin/yang symbol, the white dot in the black side and the black dot in the white side suggest that, within each polarity, there is the potential to change to the other. We are constantly flowing from yin into yang and back again as we move through our lives. Taoists speak of the importance of balancing these feminine and masculine polarities in our lives so that we may move along in life without losing our balance. Recognizing that there is a Divine Presence which is available to assist us in this process helps us to bring spirituality into our physical lives.

The Kabbalist Tree of Life is another beautiful symbol of how opposites complement one another. As in Taoism, there is a feminine side and a masculine side of the Tree of life. The Sefirot on the feminine side represent restraining qualities while those on the masculine side represent expansive ones. Sometimes it is important to give out and sometimes to receive. The feminine side offers a container, so to speak, to hold that which expands from the masculine side.

The idea of opposites working together is also noted in Sufism. Sufis are not afraid to face painful repressed memories in order to glean constructive lessons from their unconscious states of mind. When the energy (which had been used to keep those memories repressed) is brought into the light of consciousness, it may be used for more constructive purposes. This is similar to the Soul Processing techniques taught at the *Etherean Mission Application Technology* in Ghana (discussed in the New Thought chapter). Forgiveness is an important aspect of this process as well. By seeing the gifts which are available to us from experiences we have labeled as negative, we are enabled to forgive those whom we thought had hurt us in some way. By the same token, when we face things in ourselves which have been hidden, we are enabled to forgive ourselves and to transform those "negative" qualities into "positive" ones. The Sufis call this a purification process which makes our hearts worthy of housing the Beloved.

Jesus made paradoxical statements in some of the parables he used in order to teach his followers. For instance, he indicated that a person who is willing to be last will be first in God's kingdom. In other words, by helping others, a person actually helps him or herself as well. In a similar manner, in Native American cultures a person's wealth is often measured, not by the number of things acquired, but rather by the number of things given away.

In Hinduism, the notion of balancing qualities in our lives may be seen in the asanas of Hatha Yoga. These are postures which are used to balance out different energies located at various chakra points in the body. The importance of physical, emotional, mental, and spiritual alignment is stressed and practiced in this process.

In Buddhism, the idea of balance is noted in the meditation process. One sits with the back straight, focusing on the in and out breaths which occur naturally. Both are important, breathing in and breathing out. The breath symbolizes opposites working together to allow life energy to flow through our bodies, giving us life itself.

Lastly, in the New Thought Movement, it is suggested that, in order to co-create one's life experiences with the Infinite Spirit, one must put forth an intention, while also surrendering the outcome to Universal Law. This is another example of how opposite qualities work together. We do our part while Spirit does its part in co-creating the experiences of our lives.

The balancing of polarities in life gives us an opportunity to embrace both sides of the whole of any given experience. There are two sides to every coin, so to speak. We miss out on the entire experience when we focus only on one side. Metaphorically speaking, sometimes we have to experience darkness in order to appreciate the beauty of candlelight. By the same token, sometimes we have to withstand the heat of the sun in order to appreciate the coolness of the shade. By not repressing that which is hard for us to accept, we are able to see the learnings which come from all sides of a given experience.

> *Theme #6: In order to fully experience life as it is unfolding, we need to be in the present moment (Divine Presence). This makes us available to receive the gifts and opportunities from any given situation.*

As human beings, we miss out on the gifts of life, which are unfolding before our very eyes, when we dwell on the past or dream of the future.

Hindus and Buddhists address this issue by teaching meditation and mindfulness as tools for stilling the mind so that one may be fully present in the moment. Kabbalists suggest that the creation process occurs moment by moment. In order to participate in it, human beings need to be in present time. A wonderful book, written by Eckhart Tolle, entitled *The Power of Now: A Guide to Spiritual Enlightenment* (listed for you in the reference section) explores this concept in depth. I highly recommend it.

Native Americans take time to be aware of and to participate in nature's events as they occur. For example, they see the value of observing the sun as it rises and sets and they are very tuned into such things as the changing of the wind's direction and the temperature of the air. Being in the moment is a natural part of this spiritual path.

Taoists, in Tai Chi Chuan, teach the necessity of taking one conscious step at a time. They relate this to the importance of moving in a centered fashion through the changes in one's life, being fully aware of each step before taking the next one.

Jesus taught his followers to accept the wisdom of things as they are, without the need to add or subtract from them. He pointed to little children as examples of how to live fully in the present, open to the wonders of creation as it unfolds before them.

Sufis and New Thought adherents speak of bringing learnings from each experience we have in life into the present moment so that life may be fully experienced in the here and now. As mentioned before, being in the present allows us to receive the "presents" or gifts of the moment. Even those challenges which sometimes come to us in life may be viewed as opportunities for growth.

> *Theme #7: Aligning with the Divine Presence gives us an opportunity to become vessels through which divine qualities, such as peace, love, joy, compassion, gratitude, and freedom may flow through us into the world.*

This principle, if we choose to avail ourselves of it, describes how we, as human beings, may co-create our realities with the help of the Spirit Within. If we truly want to bring such qualities as peace, love, joy, and gratitude into the world, this principle lets us know that we are invited to do so. Having the faith and trust that there is a Divine Source of energy to which we, as human beings, have access, is very liberating and lets us know that we are not alone in our efforts to improve our lives.

According to the principles we have already discussed, the universe is abundant with all the resources needed to create Heaven on Earth. It seems that the challenge is in learning how to cooperate with the Divine Presence in order to bring this about. Because it would call for a global effort in order for global results to be attained, we can only begin with our personal lives. This in itself is a huge task and will require steadfast commitment on each of our parts. As has been said by many philosophers, every journey begins with the first step. We must begin at the beginning. Let us now look at how the teachings from various paths might help us in this process.

Native Americans seem to know intuitively that they are connected with that which is spiritual in life. They even recognize the spiritual essence of all forms of life, calling upon various "spirits" in nature for assistance in their efforts to sustain their lives. Similarly, African mystics or shamans might call upon the "spirits" of various organs within the body to assist in the healing process. The fact that these indigenous people might use the plural form, "spirits," to describe what others describe in the singular form, "spiritual energy," does not alter the fact that both are recognizing the spiritual essence in all of life.

We have already discussed how Taoists view the balancing of energies in life as an important step in helping one to be in tune with the universe, or Tao. Tai Chi Chuan masters have learned to direct life energy (ch'i) through their bodies, while knowing that there is a Divine Source assisting them in this process.

Hinduism offers a very special gift with regard to this principle. It is the notion that people can best help bring divine qualities into the world by choosing paths which are congruent with their natural tendencies. For instance, some people are more in touch with their mental processes and may be best suited to follow a Jnana Yoga (wisdom) path. Others, who are emotionally in tune with themselves, may be best suited for a Bhakti Yoga (devotional) path. Others, who are inclined toward caregiving, may be suited for a Karma Yoga (service) path. Still others, who are inclined toward self contemplation, may be suited for a Raja Yoga (meditation) path. Self evaluation, therefore, is an important tool to use in deciding how to cooperate with the Spirit Within.

Buddha focused on the value of developing a heart of compassion in order to create more positive life experiences for himself and others. Awakened to his oneness with all of life, he became aware of how human beings affect one another and how they may assist the Divine in bringing about Heaven on Earth.

We have already discussed how Kabbalists cooperate with the Divine in order to "raise the sparks" of divinity on earth. People on this path teach that it is our responsibility, as human beings, to help Ein Sof co-create a better world. In fact, human beings are viewed as God's arms and legs in the world.

Jesus taught his followers that God's love heals anything. In fact, he described God, the Father, as Love Itself. By choosing to co-create with God, according to this teaching, we must be alert to the guidance within which shows us how and where to channel love and compassion in our daily lives.

Sufism has been called the path of the lover. Sufis wants more than anything in the world to allow the Beloved to live through them. In Sufi

Dancing, they focus on seeing the Beloved in every face in the circle. This is a very real way of manifesting divine qualities in the world.

Within the New Thought Movement, the principle of co-creating with the Divine is an essential teaching. Human thoughts are viewed, according to this philosophy, as tools which Spirit uses in order to assist humans in bringing about positive outcomes in their lives. During this process, negative mind-sets, caught in the subconscious mind, may be brought into one's awareness so that they may be transformed (making it possible for the positive outcomes to come about).

It is appropriate and natural to thank those who assist us in our lives. It is, therefore, appropriate and natural to thank the Divine Presence in our lives for the gift of life itself. In some pathways, prayers and songs are used to praise the Divine Presence and to express gratitude for all the blessings in life. In others, appreciation for every moment as it unfolds, is, in itself, an expression of gratitude for life's gifts.

In addition to giving thanks in a verbal way, let us live our lives with hearts of gratitude for each experience as it comes our way, knowing that it is part of the grand scheme of things designed to assist us in our growth.

Author's Journey

It may be helpful for you to know how I have followed my own "inner guidance" to explore the eight paths explored in this book. I have been drawn to each of them at different times in my life in order to integrate some aspect of my life more fully. I have received gifts from each path. For instance, Native American Spirituality and African mysticism have helped me to appreciate the gifts of nature. Zen Buddhism and the Hindu chakra system have given me wonderful meditation techniques. My exposure to Spiritualism has helped me to become receptive to my own "inner teachers." Tai Chi Chuan and Hatha Yoga have helped me to become physically centered and balanced, while the Kabbalah has given me a visual map of the various parts of my personality which need to be balanced.

My discovery of the *Course in Miracles* opened my eyes to a new way of viewing Christianity, which is easier for me to accept. Sufism supports the dream work, to which I have been drawn in my association with Jungian psychology. Soul Processing has given me tools for bringing light to unconscious processes which need to be transformed. Finally, my involvement in the New Thought Movement has given me a spiritual framework which incorporates many of the various ideas I have learned from other pathways.

The Church of Religious Science and my association with an on-going women's group have given me two different settings in which to discuss and practice spiritual principles.

Discovering Your Path

It is important for individuals to tune into their own "inner guidance" when choosing spiritual practices which will be most appropriate for them. Because every person's inner journey is unique, what works best for one may not work at all for another.

We have explored eight possible avenues, each with a number of ways to connect with the Spirit Within. There are countless other paths available to us, which were not even mentioned in this book. Wayne Dyer, in his book, *Wisdom of the Ages*, points out that truths have been taught by master teachers from many walks of life throughout history. My daughter, Kerry, who is a very creative person, connects with the Spirit Within through her creative pursuits. Her approach is similar to the process Julia Cameron discusses in her book, *The Artist's Way: A Spiritual Path to Higher Creativity*.

You may decide that there are aspects from several different paths which you would like to incorporate into yours. Before you accept anything, however, be sure that it is congruent with your sense of what is true, based on your own inner experience.

Let us now turn to some suggestions which may assist you in choosing those spiritual practices most congruent with your soul's needs and which will bring you the gifts in life to which you are entitled.

One suggestion is to list the kinds of activities in your life which you enjoy the most. Then explore various spiritual practices in light of those inclinations. Do you like to sit quietly and contemplate or would you rather be up and moving? Zen Buddhism offers a beautiful form of "sitting" meditation. If you prefer more physical movement and exercise, you might consider Tai Chi Chuan, Hatha Yoga, or spending time out in nature. You may be the kind of person who gets in touch with the Spirit Within as you walk among the mountains or along the seashore. Joan Borysenko's book, *7 Paths to God: The Ways of the Mystic*, gives other helpful hints in choosing a path which is congruent with your particular interests and inclinations.

Another suggestion is to pay attention to the types of books, art, and music to which you are drawn. If you collect Native American artifacts, for example, maybe you would enjoy participating in a sweat lodge. If you are a person motivated by love and compassion, following the teachings of Jesus or Buddha may be the most appropriate path for you to follow. Perhaps you are interested in learning from your dreams. The Sufi Path offers opportunities to do dream work in order to come to know yourself better. If you are seeking a practical approach to working with Spirit in order to improve your ways of thinking about yourself and others, as well as your life experiences, you might want to consider attending one of the New Thought churches or taking Science of Mind classes. If you would like a spiritual map to help you visualize energy systems in your body, consider learning about the chakra system in Hinduism or the Tree of Life in the Kabbalist Path. When reading a book or receiving instruction in a class, be sure that you evaluate the information in the light of your own inner experience. If the information does not "feel" right to you, let it go. If it rings true, accept it as a gift.

Another suggestion is to try out some of the practice exercises in the various chapters in this book. Then ask yourself a few questions. Which exercises did I enjoy the most? Which ones helped me to learn something new about myself? Try to evaluate the exercises which helped you the most. This will give you a clue as to the kind of path to which your soul is most attuned. It might also be helpful to keep a book of daily readings, such as *Simple Abundance: A Daybook of Comfort and Joy,* by Sarah Ban Breathnach, by your bedside. Reading daily passages often reminds us to pay attention to spiritual promptings from within.

Be sure to notice the subtle and not so subtle messages which you receive when you invite your Spirit Within to guide you. Even though guidance often appears in the form of an inner "voice," as it did for Neale Walsch (*Conversations With God: An Uncommon Dialogue*), it might also appear as an intuitive hunch to follow a particular path or take a particular workshop. Maybe you are curious about something you have read and want to know more about it. Maybe you received inner pictures during meditation, when you asked Spirit to give you a message. These inner pictures probably represent something which you need to do in your life. Sometimes a song you hear on the radio or a dream image can also offer answers to the questions of your soul. I sometimes ask to be given a dream which will address a particular concern. Then I pay close attention to the symbols and messages from the dreams I receive. Although it doesn't work every time, it is very exciting and helpful when it does.

Most of us have had the experience of becoming excited while reading a particular book or listening to a particular lecture. Somehow the material just rings true for us. At other times, we quickly lose interest and put the book down or begin thinking of something else. These are inner promptings from the Spirit Within. Sometimes, I have found myself putting a book down and forgetting about it until several years later. Then suddenly I pick it up again and begin reading with a new excitement. It may be that the timing was not right before and is quite appropriate now. One such book to which I returned is Gary Zukav's, *The Seat of the Soul*. At a time when I was beginning to pay attention to inner guidance, it was helpful to read Zukav's ideas regarding "non-physical" teachers and guides.

It is important that you exercise your freedom to choose that which is appropriate for you. What is right for one person is not necessarily right for another. If you choose to join a spiritual community, be sure that it gives you the freedom of following your own "inner guidance" as you walk that path. This is very important if you want to be true to yourself.

Once you have selected those spiritual practices which work for you, make a commitment to apply them to your daily life. When you waver from your practices, however, be gentle with yourself. Don't beat yourself up emotionally just because you slipped a little. Forgive yourself as you would forgive a child who made a mistake. Then get back on the path. For instance, if you have chosen to practice a sitting form of meditation and are having trouble committing to a long period of time, try meditating for five minutes a day only. Then gradually lengthen your practice periods as you become more able to do so.

It is important to identify a pathway, to which you will be able to commit time and energy, as well as one which you will be able to incorporate into your daily life. It helps some people to become involved in a spiritual community or supportive group. If you would rather not join a group, try to identify those people in your life who will be willing to give you the support and encouragement you will need as you apply what you are learning to your life experiences.

Spirituality is not only that feeling of oneness with God, which sometimes occurs in meditation or when gazing upon something beautiful in nature, but it is the inner knowledge, on a daily basis, that we are never alone. The Divine Presence lives within each of us and is available to assist us in our journey home to our True Selves. The challenge, however, is to learn how to tune into its guidance.

As you come home to yourself more and more, you will notice that life is somehow working better for you. The resources you need tend to show up. The people you need to meet show up as well. Life becomes smoother for you and more joyful. This is how you can evaluate whether or not your spiritual path is working. May your journey home to your True Self be a wonderful experience for you. Remember that the journey never really ends, so don't forget to enjoy each step along the way!

Pamela Allen

References and Suggested Readings

References and Suggested Readings
(Arranged by Chapter)

Chapter One: Native American Spirituality

Harman, Michael. (1990). *The way of the shaman*. New York: Harper Collins.

McGaa, Ed "Eagle Man". (1990). *Mother earth spirituality: Native American paths to healing ourselves and our world*. San Francisco, CA: Harper.

Meadows, Kenneth. (1989). *Earth medicine: A shamanic way to self discovery*. Great Britain: Element Books, Limited.

Meadows, Kenneth. (1990). *The medicine way: A shamanic path to self mastery*. Great Britain: Element Books, Limited.

Medicine Eagle, Brooke. (1991). *Buffalo woman comes singing: The spirit song of a rainbow medicine woman*. New York: Ballantine Books.

Neirhart, John G., Ed. (1995). *Black Elk speaks: Being the life story of a holy man of the Oglala Sioux*. New York: William Morrow.

Ruiz, Don Miguel. (1997). *The four agreements: A Toltec wisdom book*. San Rafael, CA: Amber-Allen Pub.

Sams, Jamie (1990). *Sacred path cards: The discovery of self through native teachings*. San Francisco: Harper.

Sams, Jamie & Carson, David. (1988). *Medicine cards: The discovery of power through the ways of animals*. Santa Fe, New Mexico: Bear & Company.

Storm, Hyemeyothists. (1972). *Seven arrows*. New York: Ballantine Books.

Sun Bear, Wabun Wind, & Mulligan, Crysalis. (1991). *Dancing with the wheel: The medicine wheel workbook*. New York: Prentice Hall Press.

Sun Bear & Wabun Wind. (1980). *The medicine wheel: Earth astrology*. New York: Prentice Hall Press.

Steer, Diana. (1996). *Native American women*. New York: Barnes and Noble, Inc.

Chapter Two: Taoism

Berg, Colin. (1982). *Tales of one who seeks.* Valley Center, CA: Schofield Publishing Co.

Klein, Bob. (1984). *Movements of magic: The spirit of T'ai-Chi'Ch'uan.* North Hollywood, CA: Newcastle Publishing Co, Inc.

Klein, Bob. (1990). *Movements of power: Ancient secrets of unleashing instinctual vitality.* North Hollywood, CA: Newcastle Publishing Co. Inc.

Kuo, Simmone. (1991). *Long life good health through Tai-Chi Chuan.* Berkeley, CA: North Atlantic Books.

Lash, John. (1989). *The Tai Chi journey.* Longmead, Shaftesbury, Dorset, Great Britain: Element Books, Limited.

Lao Tsu. (1972). *Lao Tsu 's Tao te ching.* (Feng, Gia-Fu & English, Jane, Trans.). New York: Vintage Books.

Lo, Benjamin, et.al. (1985). *The essence of T'ai Chi Ch'uan: The literary tradition.* Berkeley, CA: North Atlantic Book.

Moyers, Bill. (1993). *Healing and the mind,with Bill Moyers.* (a KPBS documentary made for television). Kalamazoo, Michigan: Fetzer Institute.

Omura, Yoshiaki. (1989). Meridians, Acupuncture Points and Neurotransmitters of the Central Nervous System Localized by Bi-Digital O-Ring Test and their Relationships to Manual and Electro-Acupuncture and Qi-Gong Therapy. In the John E. Fetzer Foundation's *Energy fields in medicine: A study of device technology based on acupuncture meridians and chi energy.* (pp.395-398). Kalamazoo, Michigan: The John E. Fetzer Institute.

O'Regan, Brendan. (1989). New Paradigms in Medicine: Can They Emerge? In The John E. Fetzer Foundation's *Energy fields in medicine: A study of device technology based on acupuncture meridians and chi energy.* (pp. 230-256).Kalamazoo, Michigan: The John E. Fetzer Foundation.

Smullyan, Raymond M. (1977). *The Tao is silent.* New York: Harper & Row.

Watts, Alan, with Chung-liang Huang, Al. (1975). *Tao: The watercourse way.* New York: Pantheon Books.

Wing, R. L. (1979). *The I ching workbook.* New York: Doubleday & Co, Inc.

Chapter Three: Hinduism

Borysenko, Joan. (1997). *7 paths to God: The ways of the mystic.* Carlsbad, CA: Hay House.

Cohen, Neil S. (1988). *Chakra awareness guide.* Tarzana, CA: Legion of Light Products.

Corliss, Richard. (2001, April 23). *The power of yoga.* Time,157 (16) pp. 55-62.

Davis, Roy E. (1991). *All things possible: How to definitely experience inner peace, spiritual growth and the fulfillment of life's purposes if you sincerely want to.* Lakemont, Georgia: CSA Press.

Davis, Roy E. (1995). *Life surrendered in God: The Kriya Yoga way of soul liberation,* Lakemont, Georgia: CSA Press.

Davis, Roy E. (1997). *The self-revealed knowledge that liberates the spirit: A handbook of essential information for experiencing a conscious relationship with the infinite and restoring soul awareness to wholeness.* Lakemont, Georgia: CSA Press.

Gangaji. (1996). *Who are you: The path of self-inquiry* (an audio tape). Boulder Colorado: Sounds True.

Gangaji, (1995). *You are that!: Satsang with Gangaji.* USA: The Gangaji Foundation.

Gunther, Bernard. (1983). *Energy ecstasy: And your seven vital chakras.* North Hollywood, CA: Newcastle Publishing Company, Inc.

Hawksley, Lucinda and Whitelaw, Ian, Eds. (1995). *101 essential tips: Yoga.* New York: DK Pub. Inc.

Knott, Kim. (1998). *Hinduism: A very short introduction.* New York: Oxford Univ. Press, Inc.

Kriyananda (J. Donald Walters). (1998). *The Hindu way of awakening: Its revelation, its symbols.* Nevada City, CA: Crystal Clarity.

Leadbeater, C.W. (1980). *The chakras*. Wheaton, Illinois: Theosophical Publishing House.

Mata Amritanandamayi. (1986). *For my children: Spiritual teachings of Mata Amritanandamayi*. India: Mata Amritanandamayi Mission Trust.

Metzner, Ralph. (1971). *Maps of consciousness*. New York: Collier Books.

Myss, Caroline. (1996). *Anatomy of the spirit: The seven stages of power and healing*. New York: Three Rivers Press.

Osho. (1994). *Tantra spirituality and sex* . Boulder, Colorado: Chidvilas, Inc.

Pelikan, Jaroslav, Ed. (1992). *Sacred writings: Hinduism: The rig veda*. (Ralph T.H. Griffith, Trans.). New York: Quality Paperback Book Club.

Radice, Betty, Ed. (1962). *The Bhagavad-Gita*. (Juan Mascaro, Trans.). England: Penguin Books.

Rendel, Peter. (1986). *Introduction to the chakras*. Wellingborough, Northamptonshire: The Aquarian Press.

Sannella, Lee. (1987). *The kundalini experience: Psychosis or transcendence?* Lower Lake, CA: Integral Publishing.

Schofield, Russell P. (1982). *Joyous exploration* . Valley Center, CA: Russell Paul Schofield.

Self-Realization Fellowship. (1982). *Undreamed-of possibilities: An introduction to self-realization fellowship* . Los Angeles, CA: Self-Realization Fellowship.

Smith, Huston. (1991). *Hinduism, The world's religions: Our great wisdom traditions* (pp.12-81). San Francisco, CA: Harper.

Viswanathan, Ed. (1992). *Am I a Hindu: The Hinduism primer*. San Francisco: Halo Books.

Walters, J. Donald (Swami Kriyananda). (1996). *The path: One man's quest on the only path there is*. Nevada City, CA: Crystal Clarity Publishers.

Yogananda, Paramahansa. (1946). *Autobiography of a yogi*. Los Angeles, CA: Self Realization Fellowship.

Yogananda, Paramahansa, et.al. (1999). *A world in transition: Finding spiritual security in times of change*. Los Angeles, CA: Self Realization Fellowship.

Yogananda, Paramahansa. (1958). *Scientific healing affirmations*. Los Angeles, CA: Self Realization Fellowship.

Chapter Four: Buddhism

Bloomsbury Pub. Plc. (1999) *Encarta: World English dictionary*. (p.370). New York: St. Martins Press.

Borg, Marcus & Riegert, Ray, Eds. (1997). *Jesus and Buddha: The parallel sayings*. Berkeley, CA: Ulysses Press.

Buksbazen, John D. (1977). *To forget the self: An illustrated guide to Zen meditation*. LosAngeles, CA: Zen Center of Los Angeles.

Cooper, David A. (1992). *The heart of stillness: The elements of spiritual discipline*. New York: Bell Tower.

Elliot, William. (1995). His Holiness the Dalai Lama, *Tying rocks to clouds: Meetings and conversations with wise and spiritual people: His Holiness the Dalai Lama* (pp.120-132). Wheaton, Illinois: Quest Books.

Evans-Wentz, W.Y., Ed. (1960). *The Tibetan book of the dead*. London, Oxford, New York: Oxford University Press.

Fields, Rick, et.al. (1984). *Chop wood, carry water: A guide to finding spiritual fulfillment in everyday life*. Los Angeles, CA: Jeremy P. Tarcher, Inc.

Hagen, Steve. (1997). *Buddhism: Plain and simple*. Boston, MA: Charles E. Tuttle Co., Inc.

Hanh,Thich Nhat. (1976).*The miracle of mindfulness*. Boston: Beacon Press.

Kapleau, Philip. (1989). *The three pillars of Zen* (twenty-fifth anniversary edition) New York: Anchor Books, Doubleday. (Original work published 1965 by John Weatherhill, Inc.)

Kennett, Jiyu. (1976). *Zen is eternal life*. Emeryville, CA: Dharma Publishing.

Kopp, Sheldon B. (1972). *If you meet the Buddha on the road, kill him!* U.S. and Canada: Bantam Books.

Kornfield, Jack. (1993). *A path with heart: A guide through the perils and promises of spiritual life.* New York: Bantam Books.

Pelikan, Jaroslav, Ed. (1987). *Sacred writings : Buddhism, the Dahammapada.* (Ross Carter and Mahinda Palihawadana, Trans.). New York: Quality Paperback Book Club.

Reps, Paul and Senzaki, Nyogen. (1957, 1985). *Zen flesh, Zen bones: A collection of Zen and pre-Zen writings.* Boston: Tuttle Publishing.

Ross, Nancy W. (1980). *Buddhism: A way of life and thought.* New York: Vintage Books.

Sujata. (1987). *Beginning to see.* Berkeley, CA: Celestial Arts.

Suzuki, D.T. (1964). *An introduction to Zen Buddhism.* New York: Grove Press.

Suzuki, Shunryu. (1970). *Zen mind, beginner's mind.* New York and Tokyo: Weatherhill.

The Dalai Lama. (1995). *The power of compassion,* London: Thorsons.

Thich Nat Hanh. (1995). *Living Buddha, living Christ.* New York: Riverhead Books.

Chapter Five: Kabbalah

Bloomsbury Pub. Plc. (1999). *Encarta: World English dictionary.* (p.247). New York: St. Martins Press.

Buber, Martin. (1995).*The legend of the Baal-Shem.* Princeton, New Jersey: Princeton University Press. (originally published in 1955 by Harper & Row.)

Cooper, David. (1997). *God is a verb: Kabbalah and the practice of mystical Judaism.* New York: Berkley Publishing Group.

Epstein, Perle. (1978). *Kabbalah: The way of the Jewish mystic .* Boston, Massachusetts: Shambhala Pub., Inc.

Gonzalez-Wippler, Migene. (1987). *A Kabbalah for the modern world.* St. Paul, Minnesota: Llewellyn Publications.

Halevi, Z'ev ben Shimon. (1987). *Psychology & Kabbalah.* York Beach, Maine: Samuel Weiser, Inc.

Harvey, Andrew & Baring, Anne. (1996). *The divine feminine: Exploring the feminine face of God around the world.* Berkeley, CA: Conari Press.

Jacobson, Simon. (1996). *A spiritual guide to the counting of the omer: Forty-nine steps to personal refinement according to the Jewish tradition.* New York: Vaad Hanochos Hatmimim.

Kaplan, Aryeh. (1990). *Inner space: Introduction to Kabbalah, meditation and prophecy.* Brooklyn, New York: Moznaim Publishing Corporation.

Kaplan,Aryeh. (1995). *Sefer yetzirah: The book of creation.* Northvale, New Jersey, London: Jason Aronson, Inc.

Kramer, Sheldon Z. with Mardeene Mitchell. (2000). *Hidden faces of the soul: Ten secrets for mind/body healing from Kabbalah's lost tree of life.* Holbrook, MA: Adams Media Corp.

Kravitz, Leonard, & Olitzky, Kerry M. Eds. and Trans. (1993). *Pirke avot: A modern commentary on Jewish ethics.* New York: UAHC Press.

Matt, Daniel C. (1995). *The essential Kabbalah: The heart of Jewish mysticism.* San Francisco, CA: Harper.

Morse, Barbara H. (1961). *Squnch .* Valley Center, CA: Self Published.

Nachman, Rabbi. (1983). *Advice.* Breslov: Breslov Research Institute.

Prophet, Elizabeth C. with Spadaro, Patricia R. & Steinman, Murray. (1997). *Kabbalah: Key to your inner power.* Montana: Summit University Press.

Scholem, Gershom. (1974). *Kabbalah: A definitive history of the evolution, ideas, leading figures, and extraordinary influence of Jewish mysticism.* Jerusalem, Israel: Keter Publishing House.

Scholem, Gershom, Ed. (1949). *Zohar,the book of splendor: Basic readings from the Kabbalah.* New York: Schocken Books Inc.

Shapiro, Rami M. (1993). *Wisdom of the Jewish sages: A modern reading of pirke avot .* New York: Bell Tower.

Sheinkin, David. (1986). *Path of the Kabbalah*. St. Paul, MN: Paragon House, Pub.

Wolf, Laibl. (1999). *Practical Kabbalah: A guide to Jewish wisdom for everyday life*. New York: Three Rivers Press.

Chapter Six: Jesus and the Christ Within

Bloomsbury Pub. Plc. (1999). *Encarta: World English dictionary*. (p.762). New York: St. Martins Press.

Borg, Marcus. (1997). *Jesus and Buddha: The parallel sayings*. Berkeley, CA: Ulysses Press.

Bossis, Gabrielle. (1969). *He and I*. Quebec,Canada: Mediaspaul.

BRAVO (2000). *2000 years of Christianity*. (Made for television broadcast sponsored by American Century.)

Carey, Ken. (1985). *Terra Christa: The global spiritual awakening*. Kansas City, MO: Uni*Sun.

Eadie, Betty. (1992). *Embraced by the light*. New York: Bantam Books.

Emmerich, A. Catherine. (1983). *The dolorous passion of our Lord Jesus Christ*. Rockford, Illinois: Tan Books and Publishers, Inc.(originally published 1968.)

Emmerich, A. Catherine. (1986). *The life of Jesus Christ and biblical revelations (Vol.1)*. Rockford Illinois: Tan Books and Publishers, Inc. (originally published 1914.)

Ferrini, Paul. (1994). *Love without conditions: Reflections of the Christ mind*. U.S.A: Heartways Press.

Foundation for Inner Peace. (1992). *A course in miracles*, Glen Ellen, CA: Foundation for Inner Peace (also published in 1975 and1985.)

Fox, Matthew. (1988). *The coming of the cosmic Christ*. San Francisco: Harper & Row, Pub.

Girzone, Joseph F. (1998). *A portrait of Jesus.* New York: Image Books by Doubleday.

Green, Glenda. (1998). *Love without end: Jesus speaks.* Fort Worth, Texas: Heartwings Publishing.

Hoeller, Stephan A. (1989). *Jung and the lost gospels.* Wheaton, Ill: The Theosophical Publishing House.

Hoeller, Stephan A. (1982). *The gnostic Jung and the seven sermons to the dead.* Wheaton, Ill: Theosophical Pub. House.

King James Version (1957). *The holy bible.* London and New York: Collins' Clear-Type Press.

Larson, Martin A. (1980). *The Essene-Christian faith: A study in the sources of western religion.* Costa Mesa, CA: The Noontide Press.

Pagels, Elaine. (1981). *The gnostic gospels.* New York: Vintage Books.

Perry, Robert. (1987). *An introduction to a course in miracles.* U.S.A: Miracle Distribution Center.

Sparrow, G. Scott. (1995). *I am with you always: True stories of encounters with Jesus.* New York: Bantam Books.

Thich Nhat Hanh. (1995). *Living Buddha, living Christ.* New York: Riverhead Books.

Vaughan, Frances & Walsh, Roger. (1983,1986,1988,1995). *Gifts from a course in miracles.* New York: G.P. Putnam's Sons.

Wapnick, Gloria & Kenneth.(1987). *Awaken from the dream: A presentation of a course in miracles.* Roscoe, New York: Foundation for A Course In Miracles.

Williamson, Marianne. (1993). *A return to love: Reflections on the principles of a course In miracles.* New York: Harper Perennial.

Chapter Seven: Sufism

Barks, Coleman, Trans. (1995). *The Essential Rumi.* New York: Quality Paperback Books Club.

Cooper, David A. (2000). *Three gates to meditation practice: A personal journey into Sufism, Buddhism, and Judaism.* Woodstock, Vermont: Skylight Paths Publishing.

Ernst, Carl W. (1997). *The shambhala guide to Sufism: An essential introduction to the philosophy and practice of the mystical tradition of Islam.* Boston & London: Shambhala.

Fadiman, James & Frager, Robert, Eds. (1997). *Essential Sufism .* San Francisco: Harper.

Haeri, Fadhialia. (1990). *The elements of Sufism.* Great Britain: Element Books Limited.

Jung, C. G. (1961). *Memories, dreams, reflections.* New York: Vintage Books.

Lesser, Elizabeth. (1999). *The new American spirituality: A seeker's guide,* New York: Random House.

Lippman, Thomas W. (1995). *Understanding Islam: An introduction to the Muslim world, Second Revised Edition.* (also published 1982 and1990). New York: Meridian.

Molana Salaheddin Ali Nader Shah Angha (Pir Oveyssi). (1998). *Sufism, the reality of religion.* Riverside,CA: MTO Shahmaghsoudi Publications.

Morse, Barbara H. (1961). *Squnch .* Valley Center, CA: Self Published.

Pelikan, Jaroslav, Ed. (1984). *Sacred writings: Islam: The Qur'an.* (Ahmed Ali, Trans.) (p.301). New York: Quality Paperback Book Club.

Shah, Idries. (1964). *The Sufis.* New York: Doubleday.

Shah, Idries. (1968). *The way of the Sufi.* London: Arkana Penguin Books.

Smith, Huston. (1991). Islam, *The world's religions : Our great wisdom traditions:* (pp.221-270). Harper: San Francisco.

Vaughan-Lee, Llewellyn. (2000). *Love is a fire: The Sufi's mystical journey home.* Inverness, CA: The Golden Sufi Center.

Vaughan-Lee, Llewellyn. (1999). *The circle of love.* Inverness, CA: The Golden Sufi Center.

Vaughan-Lee, Llewellyn. (1999). *The Sufi path of love: How longing leads to the ecstasy of divine union.* (audio cassette). Boulder, Colorado: Sounds True.

Yogananda, Paramahansa. (1994). *Wine of the mystic: The rubaiyut of Omar Khayyam (A spiritual interpretation).* Los Angeles CA: Self Realization Fellowship.

Chapter Eight: New Thought Movement

Blavatsky, H.P. (1988). *The secret doctrine: The synthesis of science, religion, and philosophy.* (Vol. 1-Cosmogenesis). London: The Theosophical Publishing Company, Limited. (originally published in 1888).

Braden, Charles S. (1963, 1987). *Spirits in rebellion: The rise and development of new thought.* Dallas: Southern Methodist University Press.

Clark, Mason A. (Ed). (1982). *The healing wisdom of Dr. P. P. Quimby.* Mason Alonzo Clark: Los Altos, CA .

Emerson, Ralph W. (1926, 1951). *Emerson's essays.* (1st and 2nd Series Complete in One Vol.). New York: Harper & Row, Pub.

Holmes, Ernest. (1938,1988). *The science of mind* .(50th Anniversary Ed.). New York: G.P. Putnam's Sons. (Originally published in 1926).

Hay, Louise L. et.al. (1996). *Gratitude: A way of life.* Carlsbad, CA: Hay House, Inc.

Hay, Louise L. (1988). *Heal your body: The mental causes for physical illness and the metaphysical way to overcome them (Expanded Version).* Carson, CA. Hay House, Inc.

Hay, Louise L. (1989). *Love your body: A positive affirmation guide for loving and appreciating your body. (Expanded Version)* Carson, CA: Hay House, Inc.

Hopkins, Emma C. (date unknown). *Scientific Christian mental practice.* Marina Del Rey, CA: DeVorss & Company, Pub.

Livingood, Terry. (2000). *The bible for translating from physical to spirit.* Lee's Summit, MO: Self Published.

Myss, Caroline. (1996). *Anatomy of the spirit: The seven stages of power and healing.* New York: Three Rivers Press.

Sorensen, Christian. (1999). *Catch the spirit: Flying through life,* Del Mar,CA: Celestial Winds.

Sorensen, Christian with Marcia Hootman. (1995). *Catch the spirit: Riding the waves of life.* Del Mar, CA: Celestial Winds.

Tetteh, Ishmael N.O. (1997). *The etherean mission application technology.* (2nd Ed.) Accra,Ghana: The Etherean Mission. (originally published in 1986.)

Tetteh, Ishmael N.O. (1999). *The fountain of life: A course in metaphysics.* Accra, Ghana: The Etherean Mission. (originally published in 1975).

Tetteh, Ishmael N.O. (2001). *The inspired African mystical gospel.* (Vol.1). Accra-North, Ghana: Etherean Mission Publishing.

Trine, Ralph W. (1965). *In tune with the infinite: Fullness of peace, power and plenty.* Hammersmith, London: Thorsons. (originally published in 1899).

Troward, Thomas. (1904, 1909). *The Edinburgh and Dori' lectures.* Marina del Rey, CA: DeVorss & Co.

Conclusion

Ban Breathnach, Sarah. (1995). *Simple abundance: A daybook of comfort and joy.* New York: Warner Books.

Borysenko, Joan. (1997). *7 paths to God: The ways of the mystic.* Carlsbad, CA: Hay House.

Cameron, Julia. (1992). *The artist's way: A spiritual path to higher creativity.* New York: G. P. Putnam's Sons.

Dyer, Wayne. (1998). *Wisdom of the ages.* New York: Harper Collins.

Tolle, Eckhart. (2001). *The power of now: A guide to spiritual enlightenment .* (five unabridged audio cassettes). Novato, CA: New World Library.

Walsch, Neale. (1996). *Conversations with God: An uncommon dialogue.* New York: G. P. Putnam's Sons.

Pamela Allen

Zukav, Gary. (1989). *The seat of the soul.* New York: Simon &Schuster.

About Graphic Images

Animals pictured in Chapter One Title Page are from the Dover Clip-Art Series (1987), *Old-Fashioned Animal Cuts,* Edited by Carol Belanger Grafton. New York: Dover Publications, Inc.

Graphics for Chapters Two, Three, and Six Title Pages are from the Dover Pictorial Archive Series (1972). *Japanese Design Motifs*, Compiled by the Matsuya Piece-Goods Store. New York: Dover Publications, Inc.

Graphics for Chapter Five drawn by Rhett Miller.

Graphics for Chapter Four, Seven and Eight drawn by author.

Pamela Allen

About the Author

Dr. Pamela Allen has worked for many years to address educational and psychological needs of children and adults. Realizing that education and psychology are limited in their ability to address the deeper needs of the soul, she decided to write *Awakening to the Spirit Within*. It introduces eight sacred paths, all of which were part of Dr. Allen's own spiritual journey. She now uses it as a text for teaching spiritual principles.

Dr. Allen earned her master's degree in special education from the University of Florida and her doctorate in psychology from the United States International University. She lives in Southern California, where she enjoys traveling and spending time with her family and friends.

www.ingramcontent.com/pod-product-compliance
Lightning Source LLC
Chambersburg PA
CBHW030310290526
45785CB00001B/290